BOB DYLAN IN LONDON
TROUBADOUR TALES

JACKIE LEES AND K G MILES

Published by McNidder & Grace
21 Bridge Street
Carmarthen
SA31 3JS
Wales, UK

www.mcnidderandgrace.com

First published in 2021
© Jackie Lees and K G Miles

All rights reserved. No part of this work may be reproduced or transmitted in any form or by any means, electronic or mechanical, including photocopy, recording, or any information storage or retrieval system, without permission in writing from the publisher.

Jackie Lees and K G Miles have asserted their right to be identified as the authors of this work in accordance with the Copyright, Designs and Patents Act 1988.

Every effort has been made to obtain necessary permission with reference to copyright material. The publisher apologises if, inadvertently, any sources remain unacknowledged and will be glad to make the necessary arrangements at the earliest opportunity.

A catalogue record for this work is available from the British Library.

Illustrations (listed on p. 111) © Julia Wytrazek

ISBN: 9780857162144
Ebook: 9780857162151

Designed by JS Typesetting Ltd, Porthcawl
Cover design: Lara Peralta
Cover illustration: Julia Wytrazek

Printed and bound in the United Kingdom by Short Run Press Ltd, Exeter, UK

Praise for *Bob Dylan in London*

'The ultimate guide to Dylan in London; informative, entertaining and essential.'
David Quantick, music writer

'Meticulously researched and packed with delicious detail, this highly enjoyable book reveals both Bob Dylan and London in all of their compelling originality. With wry observation and entertaining incident, this is the story of Dylan's earliest visits to London as an unknown folk singer, crashing in friends' bedsits, right through to his sell-out concerts at the Royal Albert Hall and Earls Court.'
Conor McPherson, playwright, *Girl from the North Country*

'London had a big influence on the young Bob Dylan… it's all in this wonderful book Bob Dylan in London. And as an avid Dylan fan even I learnt something new. I heartily recommend it.'
George Galloway, politician, broadcaster and writer

'There is no doubt that Bob Dylan loves London. He has played numerous concerts there and had many adventures too, notably the renowned story of him trying to find Dave Stewart's studio in Crouch End. It is great that Jackie Lees and KG Miles have put all the locations together. I may not always be able to visit them, but at least I can do it in my mind with the help of this book.'
Spencer Leigh, BBC broadcaster and author of *Bob Dylan: Outlaw Blues*

'A nice, easy to read yet informative journey around Dylan's London that takes in nearly sixty years of Bob's visits to England's capital. Much more than just a walking guide.'
Derek Barker, author, magazine editor and music historian

'The Troubadour, where Dylan played in 1962 on his first trip out of America, the Royal Festival Hall, the Royal Albert Hall, venues of the mid-1960s masterpiece performances before and after "going electric", the triumphant return to Earl's Court in 1978, and Camden Town, scene of a 1993 Dylan stroll and photo session.

These are just some of the places in this endlessly invigorating city to which Jackie Lees and KG Miles take us in Bob Dylan in London: Troubadour Tales, *their highly readable and essential archaeological tour through Bob Dylan's London, a city that has always been dear to him.'*
Professor Richard F. Thomas, Harvard University and author of *Why Dylan Matters*

'An essential purchase for anyone who loves Dylan, or London, or both.'
★ ★ ★ ★ ★ ***Record Collector***

Dedicated to the memory of Steve Walsh, a Dylan fan so long as someone else was singing, and to Zoe Lees Walsh, definitely not a Dylan fan, but there's plenty of time.

To Cathy and Issy and Roy, without whom I 'couldn't even find the door'

CONTENTS

Foreword by Andrew Muir — ix

Introduction — 1
Chapter 1: Folk Clubs — 5
Chapter 2: 9 Tregunter Road — 21
Chapter 3: The May Fair — 33
Chapter 4: The Savoy — 45
Chapter 5: Savoy Steps — 57
Chapter 6: Royal Albert Hall — 67
Chapter 7: Earls Court and Blackbushe — 81
Chapter 8: Camden Town and Crouch End — 95
Afterword — 107

List of illustrations — 111

Map (see colour section)

Locations list	113
Bibliography	121
Acknowledgements	125
Author biographies	129

Foreword
LONDON CALLING

The story of Bob Dylan's life and career winds its way through the streets of London from his first arrival in December 1962 to, so far, his last appearance, headlining a festival, at Hyde Park on July 12th 2019.

I am honoured to be asked to write this foreword, and I have great pleasure in doing so as I have seen Dylan more times in London than any other city, more, indeed, than the next few combined. To follow London's intersections with Bob Dylan is to throw into high relief this mercurial artist's restless and explorative genius over the last six decades.

In Dylan's 2003 movie *Masked and Anonymous* Jeff Bridges' character has a rant about "The Empire is finished." Dylan, in the 21st century, often refers to past empires, such as Roman and English, to comment on the American one of the present day. Or even as in this case, the future, where the focus is London: 'You got Big Ben and the Tower, but it's just a theme park. Sheesh, you got your start there, how does that make you feel, that the Empire is finished?' As ever in Dylan's later art, the truth is presented askew. Whilst not being historically correct, it can tell us what Dylan sees as historically significant, even in fictionalised settings.

While not 'getting his start there', a trip to London in the early 1960s proved pivotal, coming as it did in between his low-key debut album, consisting mainly of covers, and the astonishing declaration of his song-writing genius on his second album, *The Freewheelin' Bob Dylan*. Given Dylan's lack of status at the time, the fact that he had been flown from New York to London to appear in a play for TV, *Madhouse on Castle Street*, as recounted here, was extraordinary. A suitable foreshadowing of a career that would be full of surprises. Dylan's first arrival in London found it in the grip of one of the coldest winters on record, thereby neatly mirroring his first arrival in New York City.

A hugely influential Festival Hall concert in 1964 was followed by visits in 1965 and 1966 that have been immortalised on film. That famous precursor to promo videos to promote 'Subterranean Homesick Blues' was filmed in the London alleyway known as the Savoy Steps Hotel as detailed in chapter 5. The documentaries

Dont Look Back and *Eat the Document* catch Dylan in London as he moves from folk to electric rock and the subsequent brouhaha that followed this. You see Dylan in the Carnaby Street of Swinging London, and if you follow the outtakes, you witness a very ill Dylan and a worried John Lennon trying to jolly things along as they are driven along the side of the river Thames.

The cameras provide us with many unforgettable images of Dylan at the centre of a merry-go-round that is going ever faster until the wheels come off and, then for London, there is a long, long gap until 1978. By that time, I am old enough for my personal Dylan tale to become entwined with 'Dylan-in-London'.

The London 1978 shows are a thing of legend, forming pivotal episodes in the lives of many thousands who had grown up with the music but never seen the man perform it. It started for me by queueing for tickets in Glasgow. I remember the London paper, the *Evening Standard*, filled with page after page after page of classified adverts, consisting of Dylan tickets both wanted and for sale. Touts had mingled with the fans and tickets were now being offered at exorbitant prices. A vast open-air venue, Blackbushe Aerodrome, was added to the European leg of the tour to ameliorate the situation. As for me, I had the maximum allocation of six tickets: five for myself and one for my friend, Dave Wingrove, who was generously putting me up for the week. The agonies I went through on the night I missed are as indescribable as the pleasures of the nights I attended.

Many years later, at a Dylan convention, I met a woman who had, coincidentally, sat in front of me on a bus back to Scotland from London. Her memories of me on that trip were crystal clear, as she described me as 'the most excited person I've ever seen in my life, and this was a few days after the concert had finished.' I never thought I could come anywhere near being that excited again. However, as this book recounts, 15 years later, in London once again, this was proven to be incorrect.

Dylan returned to Earl's Court in 1981 and topped the bill at a sold-out Wembley in scorching weather in 1984. He was back in London in 1987 and 1989, by which time I was living in London. These two years were respectively his last in London before the "Never-Ending Tour" began, and his first of so very many on it.

Just before the new decade began, I moved to within a short walk of Hammersmith Odeon. Erm, *coincidentally*, Dylan started the year with a string of shows there, a feat he repeated the following year. He then added another residency at the same venue in 1993, and he kept coming back after that, too.

The 1990s: living in Fulham, running my own Dylan fanzine, with Himself regularly visiting nearby and, consequently, a constant stream of Dylan loving friends and family sleeping on the floor and mass meetings of Dylanistas at local hotels, year after year. No wonder these London times were my happiest Bob days.

After Dylan's last visit of the decade to London, I left the city; but I only moved an hour's travelling distance away, as we went into the new century, new millennium and Dylan returned to London to grace Wembley Arena. The same venue witnessed the following onstage speech, prompted, no doubt, by the backstage gift of a photographic book recalling London in the Blitz:

We're playing over here with a lot of pride, it's a big honour to play in this country, Great Britain. When I grew up, they used to tell me about the Battle of Britain, RAF, Winston Churchill, all that stuff. Now, we all know that Britain stood alone and without any allies; and that always meant a lot to me and everybody that I grew up with.

Dylan was back in London in 2003 and performed 'Romance in Durango' for the only time thus far, since 1976. 2005 also brought set-list surprises when he ended the year's touring with a five-night residency at Brixton. Particularly relevant here was a cover of 'London Calling' with the Clash's Mick Jones in the audience.

From 2003 onwards, Dylan has played in London every couple of years, including triumphant returns to the Royal Albert Hall, culminating in Hyde Park in 2019. In 2020 the Coronavirus pandemic halted Dylan's yearly touring, which stretches back, unbroken even by a serious illness in 1997, all the way to 1986. We all fervently hope that circumstances change and allow him to get back on the road to showcase songs from his new album, *Rough and Rowdy Ways* and to play live, once again, in London.

Andrew Muir, 2020

INTRODUCTION

This book will take you on a journey through London, following in the footsteps of Bob Dylan from the first time he set foot in the capital in the winter of 1962.

We begin in December 1962 with the London folk clubs where 21-year-old, and largely unknown, Dylan received a mixed reception. North London's tiny King and Queen pub claims to be the first place that Dylan ever sang publicly outside the USA – a claim that will be examined in some detail. The other contenders are the Princess Louise, often listed in the top 10 buildings to visit in London, and the Water Rats at Kings Cross. Both venues were home to the Singers' Club where the young Dylan enthralled and irritated in equal measure an audience unused to the voice and style of the American outsider. We'll also call in to the Troubadour club in Earls Court, now home to the Dylan Room in honour of his well-documented performances in its dark and atmospheric basement on that first visit.

Moving on from the folk clubs, we'll pop around the corner from the Troubadour and visit number 9, Tregunter Road, where Dylan met up with some American friends on that first trip to the UK. It was here that he had an encounter with legendary writer Robert Graves, a meeting which may have changed his whole career.

Next stop on the journey is the luxurious May Fair hotel. In 1962 the BBC was paying the bill as Dylan was to star in a TV drama. He didn't like the rules or the formality and was moved to the Cumberland, which although more to his taste, did not stop him spending more time hanging out with new friends and acquaintances than bedding down there. It was a very different Dylan who later stayed at the May Fair during his legendary 1966 'electric' tour.'

From the May Fair, the journey will take you to another hotel, this time the Savoy. The hotel's hospitality may have been strained by Dylan's stay in 1965 during which he was accompanied by a film crew as well as various friends and an ex-lover. Not to mention the numerous guests who popped by to pay court. Not all behaved well.

Hidden away behind the Savoy hotel is a small alley, the next stop in our tour. Our story here recounts the making of the first ever music video, filmed in Savoy Steps. Many people assume that the filming of the video for 'Subterranean Homesick Blues' took place in New

York, when in fact film maker D A Pennebaker shot three versions in and around the Savoy.

Illustrating just how much Dylan's relationship to London changed between his first and second visits to the capital, the next locations we visit are the Royal Festival Hall, where Dylan performed a solo concert in 1964, and the Royal Albert Hall, site of extraordinary concerts in both 1965 and 1966. It's debatable whether the leap from 1962 to 1964 was ever as big as the one he took between 1964 and 1966, when he 'went electric' and acquired a backing band – not just any band, but The Band.

It was 12 more years before Dylan was to return to London. We pick up the trail at the site of those long-awaited concerts at Earls Court's Exhibition Centre. Never an inspiring building even in its heyday, it hosted those eagerly anticipated gigs. Their huge success led to an extra event being scheduled – the Picnic in the Park at Blackbushe, which we'll also visit.

Our journey through London comes to an end with Dylan's 1998 trip to Camden Town and Crouch End in North London. Camden was the location for filming the video for 'Blood In My Eyes', the stand-out track on the wonderful *World Gone Wrong* album. Crouch End, a short bus ride away, has its own story to tell, perhaps a little more fanciful than some of the others stories of Dylan's encounters with London, but certainly entertaining.

This book relates the stories of each landmark location and its significance in the career of the artist who is surely the most important songwriter of the latter half of the 20th century. You can take the trip for yourself – a pilgrimage of sorts perhaps – and call in to the pubs, clubs, cafes, hotels, streets and venues where Dylan left his mark, and was marked in return by many of them.

London was never just a regular destination, or another stop on the world tour. It was always more than that.

Chapter 1
FOLK CLUBS

Bob Dylan first came to London in the freezing December of 1962. Snow blanketed the capital from December to February 1963, and mini icebergs were seen on the river Thames. Only the winters of 1683–84 and 1739–40 were colder than 1962–63. Dylan came to take part in a television play, and while he was in town, he visited a lot of London's folk clubs. At that time, he was a relative unknown in the UK, although some folk music fans might have noticed his face on the cover of American folk magazine *Sing Out!* and seen copies of his lyrics inside. His first album, *Bob Dylan*, had not sold well, and his breakthrough second, *The Freewheelin' Bob Dylan*, was yet to come.

The London folk scene that he encountered was factionalised and critical, in sharp contrast to the buzzing and overwhelmingly welcoming one he had left behind in New York's Greenwich Village.

The main folk rivalry in America was between cities – Boston versus New York – rather than within the same city as was the case in London. In Boston, musicians like Eric Von Schmidt were interested in ethnic authenticity, the recreation of old blues, country and bluegrass. In contrast, New York was more political, as personified by Pete Seeger and The Weavers.

Joe Boyd, a manager at the Newport Folk Festival and later head of Hannibal Records in London, said: 'The point in New York was to sing that same song in exactly the same style in which you would sing a Spanish Civil War song and a cowboy song, to emphasise the brotherhood of all men, and to make it easy for the masses to sing along.'

In London, songs from the British tradition had dominated the folk repertoire in the 1950s, but although the likes of 'The Wild Rover' and 'The Leaving of Liverpool' were still mandatory fare, audiences were open to a wide range of material.

Factions had started to appear, each holding strong opinions – not just about which songs were legitimate to sing, but the way in which they should be sung. Some decreed that all folk songs should be sung unaccompanied, frowning upon the use of musical instruments. Others considered that only songs from the British Isles were acceptable. The policy at the influential Singers' Club, started by Ewan MacColl as the Ballad and Blues Club in 1953, was that songs should be from the singer's own heritage or region of birth. It should be said, though, that some singers, such as Martin Carthy, largely ignored such rigid rules.

Into this fractious London folk scene sauntered the young Bob Dylan, in his cowboy boots.

Dylan's first appearance at a London folk club was on 21 December 1962 at the King and Queen, at number 1 Foley Street in Fitzrovia. The pub had been a haunt of another Dylan, the poet Dylan Thomas. To this day it continues to host a folk club in a small bar upstairs.

On the night Bob Dylan set foot in the King and Queen, Martin Carthy was playing as a member of the Thameside Four. Looking out at the audience he saw a face he recognised from the cover of *Sing Out!*. Carthy walked over to the visitor and said, 'You're Bob Dylan', then asked him to sing later. 'We carried on with the evening for about 20 minutes and he just looked up at me from the audience and nodded, so I called him up.'

> Dylan's first appearance at a London folk club was on 21 December 1962 at the King and Queen, on 1 Foley Street in Fitzrovia
>
> **Map ref. 4**

As Carthy recalls: 'The audience knew they were watching something that was really good. Anybody who says anything different is talking through their hat. The audience loved him. He did three songs and they demanded an encore. He was great, very funny and very dry. He spoke a little to the audience, not a lot, just a little – but he never did talk to the audience that much.'

The King and Queen still has a photo on the wall of that December night, taken by folk archivist Brian Shuel. Guitar in hand, harmonica in mouth, flat cap … already a very recognisable figure is looking out at us.

There was another notable legacy of that gig. Don McLean's classic song 'American Pie' chronicles the growth of popular music. He sings: 'Now, for ten years we've been on our own' – a ten-year span that takes music from Alan Freed's inception of rock and roll in 1952 until this appearance of Dylan in London in 1962. As the song continues, McLean remembers the time '[when] the Jester sang for the king and queen / In a coat he borrowed from James Dean / And a voice that came from you and me'. In the song, Dylan is the jester, the only person at court able to speak candidly to those in power.

He can be seen wearing that James Dean coat on the cover of *Freewheelin'*.

On the King and Queen's website is a note that *Time Out* magazine listed Dylan's performance of three songs in their tiny club in that winter of 1962 as one of the 50 most important gigs of all time.

Martin Carthy befriended Dylan, and the two spent time together, including a memorable evening at Carthy's London home in Hampstead, where a piano was attacked with an axe to provide firewood. In 1984, speaking of his first London visit, Dylan recalled running into people who knew a lot about traditional English folk songs, and acknowledged that he had learned a lot from Carthy.

Carthy taught Dylan both 'Scarborough Fair' and 'Lady Franklin's Lament', a 19th-century ballad commemorating the death of Sir John Franklin. These two English songs would prove important for the *Freewheelin'* album.

The night after performing at the King and Queen, Dylan played at the Singers' Club Christmas party at the Pindar of Wakefield (now the Water Rats) in Grays Inn Road. The folk club was in an upstairs bar at the pub, and a photograph of that night, also taken by Brian Shuel, shows a packed venue of attentive folk fans, mostly in suits.

At some point earlier that day, Dylan had been told to 'f— off' after being caught smoking pot at the Roundhouse. When he arrived at the Pindar of Wakefield, the doorman, who had heard about the incident, said: 'I don't want to let that shit in.' Pete Seeger, leading light of the American folk scene, came to Dylan's defence and got him in.

Seeger had first met the 19-year-old Dylan at the bedside of Seeger's friend, and Dylan's idol, Woody Guthrie. Guthrie's health was by then deteriorating due to Huntington's disease, from which he eventually died in 1967. Seeger championed the young Dylan and their paths had crossed many times in New York before they ran into each other in London.

At the Singers' Club, Dylan sang 'Masters of War' and the 'Ballad of Hollis Brown'. Not everyone was impressed. Peggy Seeger, Pete's half-sister and Ewan MacColl's girlfriend, said: 'Somebody's whispered: "Bob Dylan's here", and I seem to remember saying: "Who is Bob Dylan?" I didn't really know who he was but I do remember he was very withdrawn and when he stood up to sing he made literally no impression because you couldn't hear him. But he did one song, and stepped down.' She admitted later that perhaps they could have been more welcoming.

Some commentators have maintained that Dylan's first appearance outside America was at the Singers' Club, but Martin Carthy bears witness that Dylan's first performance on a UK stage was indeed at the King and Queen on 21 December. After the performance that evening, Dylan stayed with Carthy and the two discussed the Singers' Club and the Troubadour as venues Dylan should play.

Accepting that his second gig was at the Singers' Club, there has been much confusion over the years about the exact location of that club on 22 December 1962.

The Ballad and Blues Club was originally held at the Princess Louise in Holborn. By the time it was renamed as the Singers' Club in 1961, it was located in a trade union building, from where it moved to a variety of pubs, including the Pindar of Wakefield.

There are a number of photographs by Brian Shuel of that second Dylan gig in London on 22 December, but the location is unattributed. Ever since, there has been speculation about a number of possible venues. However, another Brian Shuel photograph, of folk singer Anne Briggs at the Singers' Club in 1962, is attributed to the Pindar of Wakefield. Behind Briggs is a very distinctive wallpaper – the same wallpaper seen behind Dylan at the Christmas gig.

Each time the Singers' Club moved, Ewan MacColl added a new verse to his 'Ballad of the Travels', a humorous song which documented the life of the club. In this way we know that the Singers' Club was at the Pindar of Wakefield for two years, and more than likely at the time that Dylan played. Or, in the words of Ewan MacColl in his song,

> The Pindar it became oor hame
> For twa long years we kept it
> Till the landlord there gave us the air
> And then by Christ we left it.

* * *

During his visit to London in the winter of 1962–1963, Dylan also played or visited a number of the coffee house venues that had grown up in London after the Second World War, most notably the Troubadour.

Mike and Sheila Van Bloemen had arrived in London from Montreal in 1952 with only the ability, according to a friend, to 'make scrambled eggs and a good coffee'. They wanted to run a coffee house, and with money borrowed from, among others, the writer Robert Graves, they opened the Troubadour on Brompton Road in Earls Court in 1954. The Van Bloemens ran the Troubadour until 1972, their children growing up in the flat upstairs.

The Troubadour was the first of many to combine coffee shop, meeting place and music venue. Bruce Rogerson, a regular from that time and future owner of the Troubadour, says, 'Mike and Sheila were intellectuals, well educated. They made it a place where you could relax, which had a lot more to offer than a Lyons Tea House. It was a café in the European sense, right from the start.'

The Troubadour, home to the Dylan Room since 2019, was and still is a coffee shop at street level, with a walled garden at the back. In the narrow basement is a club that holds just over 100 people comfortably, but which has held many more at times over the years. In the club, only the position of the stage has really changed since the early 1960s: entering the Troubadour in the 21st century is like stepping back in time.

Throughout the 1960s and '70s, the Troubadour was a musical and literary centre in London. Paul Simon played the venue many times as he honed his craft in the early '60s. Jimi Hendrix played there in 1966 when he arrived in London as an unknown. It was also the first home of the satirical magazine *Private Eye*.

The folk singer Sandy Denny often performed at the Troubadour. Her biographer wrote that 'once through the heavily ornate street door, you've a feeling of entering another country, another time. It's one of the most extraordinary pockets of eccentricity in London. You have good and bad nights there but never a visit when nothing of consequence happens.' Besides being a singer, Denny was a nurse at a nearby hospital. It has been said that she sometimes provided drugs to the regulars to make the evening go even better. Dylan was certainly introduced to a greater array of drugs than had been available in Greenwich Village during his visits to the folk clubs in London.

> His first appearance on the Troubadour's basement stage was on 29 December 1962, when he sang 'Death of Emmett Till', 'Ballad of Hollis Brown' and – to the surprise of Martin Carthy – a song that was based on the folk standard Lord Randall.
> **Map ref. 14**

Just around the corner from the Troubadour is Tregunter Road, where Dylan stayed for a number of nights that chilly winter with his old friends Richard Farina and Eric von Schmidt.

His first appearance on the Troubadour's basement stage was on 29 December 1962, when he sang 'Death of Emmett Till', 'Ballad of Hollis Brown' and – to the surprise of Martin Carthy – a song that was based on the folk standard Lord Randall.

'Lord Randall' is a ballad that consists of a dialogue between a young Lord and his mother. Through the mother's inquiry, it is gradually revealed that the Lord has been poisoned by his lover, who has fed him poisoned eels. Carthy recalled, 'He started, "Where have you been my blue-eyed son" … and I'm thinking, *Oh he's going to sing "Lord Randall"*. But that line was where the similarity with "Lord Randall" ended. He just took off on this great song, "Hard Rain". And in 1962 that song was revolutionary.'

Some have suggested that the Cuban Missile Crisis of October 1962 was the inspiration for 'A Hard Rain's A-Gonna Fall', but the fact that his first public performance of the song was a month before the crisis occurred seems to rule that out.

During this time in London, Dylan also visited a number of other folk clubs on the London scene, but it's unlikely he sang at any of them. One was Bunjies at 27 Litchfield Street, just off Charing Cross Road in the West End. Another of the original 1950s' coffee house and folk clubs, this was another basement venue, and a tiny one at that. It was, in fact, a 400-year-old wine cellar. Allegedly named after the first owner of the club's pet hamster, it was an early venue for both Rod Stewart and David Bowie. A sign on the door read 'for our sake and yours, close the bluddy door'. Once a vibrant part of the London music scene, it is now a Moroccan restaurant.

Another club Dylan visited was Les Cousins (generally pronounced Lez Cuzzins) at 49 Greek Street. This club in the very heart of Soho had been one of the most important music venues in the early years of popular music, when it was known as the Skiffle Cellar. It closed in 1972.

Also on Greek Street, at Number 18, was the newly opened Establishment Club, a nightclub co-founded by British comedian Peter Cook, which Dylan is said to have visited. Its status as a nightclub allowed comedians and satirists to perform material that might otherwise have fallen foul of censorship laws. It was short-lived, closing in 1964.

He also ventured as far as the Surbiton and Kingston Folk Club, which lasted rather longer, until 1977.

Dylan would perform one more time on a London stage before going back to the USA. In the meantime, on 5 January 1963, he flew with his manager, Albert Grossman, to Rome to support Odetta, another of Grossman's protégées on her tour. They were joined by Mary Travers of Peter, Paul and Mary. While abroad he worked with 'Scarborough Fair', one of the tunes he'd learned from Martin Carthy.

On Dylan's return to London five days later, Martin Carthy received a surprise: 'When [Dylan] came back from Italy, he'd written "Girl from the North Country";

he came down to the Troubadour and said, "Hey, here's 'Scarborough Fair' and he started playing this thing."'

On 12 January 1963, after an aborted attempt to infiltrate a college party with two college students, Dylan, Richard Farina and Eric Von Schmidt headed back to the Troubadour.

Judy Silvers, an Israeli singer, was playing when they arrived. 'Now there's something you don't see every day,' said Dylan, 'a Jewish folksinger.' After listening for a while, Dylan and his friends decided to get up and play. Silvers was reluctant to let go of the stage; after all, she was the paid act for the evening, but eventually she conceded that they could have seven minutes during her break. She didn't make it back on.

Dylan, Farina and Von Schmidt were joined on the tiny stage by Martin Carthy and Ethan Signer, an American fiddle player. Iconic photos taken by Alison Chapman McLean show a joyous ensemble. The photographs can be seen on the Richard Farina fansite.[1]

Dylan played a couple of songs alone. The first was the as yet unrecorded 'Don't Think Twice It's Alright', with a rather drug-befuddled Dylan staring at his guitar-picking fingers, exclaiming: 'My fingers are moving soooo sloooow' and then looking up and saying: 'Where are we … underwater? Are we in a submarine?' In one of the more surreal heckles in music

---

1. http://www.richardandmimi.com/troubadour.html

history, someone shouted: 'This is no submarine. This is Mayfair!' The heckler was clearly no geography student: the Troubadour is in Earls Court, not Mayfair.

'Are you a fish?' asked Dylan, who then went on to give a perfect rendition of the song, followed by a stunning 'Blowin' in The Wind'.

Not all the hecklers were benign. One was the Scottish musician Nigel Denver, who had fallen out with Dylan. According to Anthea Joseph, who ran the Troubadour at the time, 'It was [over] the fact he considered Bob couldn't sing his way out of a paper bag, couldn't play a guitar, and couldn't play a harp, and that Nigel was infinitely better.'

Before Dylan returned home, the Troubadour group gathered on 14 and 15 January in the basement of Dobell's Jazz Record Shop to record a short set (19 minutes) of folk songs. Dylan was wary of recording under his own name, so he opted for the pseudonym Blind Boy Grunt. It was one he was to use a number of times.

As an aside, on *The Basement Tapes*, recorded in 1967, is a song called 'Open The Door, Homer'. Homer was the nickname of Richard Farina. Despite the song title, and all the official and unofficial books insisting the lyric to be 'Open the Door, Homer', it is clear that Dylan is singing 'Open The Door, Richard'. Consciously or subconsciously, was Dylan trying to recreate the fun and exciting jam sessions with Richard Farina and Eric

> Consciously or subconsciously, was Dylan trying to recreate the fun and exciting jam sessions with Richard Farina and Eric Von Schmidt at those other basements, in Dobells Record Store and the Troubadour?
>
> **Map ref. 5**

Dylan had begun recording his second album, *Freewheelin'*, nine months before he came to London in 1962. It wasn't finished until a few months after he returned to the USA. Then it became a huge success, reaching Number 1 in the UK album charts in 1964. It contained two songs that owed a direct debt to his time in London, and Martin Carthy in particular. One was 'Girl from the North Country', and the other was Bob Dylan's 'Dream', inspired by Carthy's rendition of 'Lady Franklin's Lament'.

Dylan's time in the folk clubs of London was short but frenetic. He took so much and he changed so much, stirring up the scene a little. He returned to the USA with a renewed dynamism and a few new tunes in his bag.

Even after the success of *Freewheelin'*, the London folk scene was suspicious and often dismissive of Dylan. UK folk magazine *Sing*, in print until 1974, regarded Dylan as a controversial figure, leading a 'new wave'. They pointed out that his growing commercial success meant that 'the knives were sharpened and the folk world split into violently pro and anti-Dylan camps.' *Sing* also noted that most were still in the anti-Dylan camp, and advised that his 'writing talents are weakening'!

In the same magazine, Nigel Denver made it clear which camp he was in, criticising one of Dylan's songs as a 'nonsensical piece of rubbish'. Nigel gave young Bob the following advice: 'Stop churning out songs. When you write one, work on it and get it perfect'.

But he gave some words of encouragement too:

'I don't see any reason if you die of old age why you should not make a contribution to folk music.'

Chapter 2
9 TREGUNTER ROAD

The years have not been kind to Earls Court's Old Brompton Road, home to the Troubadour folk club, and the application for gentrification has clearly been lost in the post.

However, should you walk away from the main thoroughfare, you suddenly find yourself – without any sign or fanfare – in the tree-lined roads of Chelsea, where you breathe the distinct air of affluence. Suddenly, the price tags have quadrupled, even for an annexe. It's here that you will find 9 Tregunter Road, a house that in the early 1960s would hold the key to a critical chapter of Bob Dylan's story.

The area has always housed the extremely wealthy side by side with the bohemian and cosmopolitan. Little of this cultural and financial juxtaposition has changed from when a young Dylan found himself wandering these streets, suitcase in one hand, guitar in the other, during the icy winter of 1962.

On New Year's Eve of that year, as Dylan and Martin Carthy were singing 'Auld Lang Syne' at the King and Queen in Central London, two Americans were flying into London to record an album. Richard Farina (later to add the tilde to his name and become Fariña) and Eric Von Schmidt were friends of Dylan from New York. Von Schmidt was a folk club legend once described by Dylan as 'a man who can sing the bird off the wire and the rubber off the tyre'. On his first album, Dylan covered his 'Baby, Let Me Follow You Down'.

Farina had a record deal for which he had looked to Von Schmidt for collaboration. They also had notions of producing a film, the plot of which revolved around a trippy cowboy, a role that intrigued a young Dylan, who spoke to them about a role for himself as a wandering maverick.

Farina was also writing a book which would become a '60s cult classic, *Been Down So Long It Looks Like Up to Me*. He would later marry Joan Baez's sister, Mimi.

Needing a place to stay, Farina and Von Schmidt contacted Rory McEwen, someone they knew through the folk music scene. On arriving in London, they moved into Number 9, the McEwen family's elegant Chelsea town house.

Rory was an Eton-educated polymath and son of an extremely wealthy and well-connected family. Then a poet and a folk singer, he would go on to become a renowned nature artist. Inspired by Huddie William Ledbetter, better known as Lead Belly, he was the first person to play 12-string acoustic guitar on British TV. He also hosted the pioneering BBC music show *Hullaballoo*, which featured young hopefuls such as Van Morrison and Billy Connolly.[1] Interestingly, the format for this innovative show is the same now used, many years later, by the son-in-law he never met, the musician and TV presenter Jools Holland.

The two Americans settled easily into the comfortable grand parlour of Number 9. After a while, Farina asked Von Schmidt if he had noticed that although they never washed up any of the dishes, they were always clean, and that the end of the toilet paper was always folded neatly and the towels in the bathroom were always warm? He wondered if there was an invisible butler living with them to cater for their every need. Unfortunately for them, a very real butler would eventually materialise.

They began to circulate around the London folk clubs, frequenting the Troubadour in particular. Tregunter Road was so close to the club that you could almost hear a banjo being tuned. One day in early January 1963, the manager of the Troubadour, Anthea Joseph, mentioned to them that Dylan was in town.

---

1. *Hullabaloo* was a folk and R&B showcase broadcast late on Saturday nights to the north of England only. The series ran on ABC TV from 1963 to 1964, each half-hour show featuring British and American folk and blues artists.

Without an address or telephone number for him, Farina left a message with Anthea: 'Von Schmidt and I are here to make a record. Come to the McEwen's pad. Free beer.'

Later that same week Dylan found the note and made his way the few hundred yards to Number 9, where he was greeted by Von Schmidt. After a frosty few minutes (his trademark), he asked if Von Schmidt wanted to hear a song he'd written. He then played a fully formed rendition, one of the very first, of 'Don't Think Twice, It's Alright'.

Number 9 had become a creative hub on the folk circuit under the McEwens, and throughout that day it slowly filled with musicians and partygoers. The kitchen was commandeered and a bean stew prepared. Von Schmidt had everyone stomping and hooting to the blues.

Dylan and Von Schmidt tried to outdo each other on the harmonica. Farina and Dylan got stoned, enjoying their access to more exciting drugs than they'd had back home. As well as drugs, the 21-year-old Dylan was also getting a taste for Gordon's Gin and cheeseburgers from the local Wimpy Bar.

The party lasted for three days. One night, while the party was in full swing, Dylan met the legendary poet and writer Robert Graves. It was a meeting that would profoundly change the young Dylan, both artistically and personally.

The McEwen family, in particular Rory, were close friends of the Graves family. Robert Graves was a literary giant, known around the world for his novel *I, Claudius* and for his memoir of the First World War, *Goodbye to All That*. His obituary in the *New York Times* notes that 'his range of subject matter was staggering. Prehistoric Greece, the life of Imperial Rome, Cromwellian England, revolutionary America ... ' It was a versatility the young Dylan would surely have admired.

Graves had published *The White Goddess* in 1948. This mixture of history, poetry and philosophy suggested that true poetry stemmed from an ancient female muse. His ideas of poetic inspiration and the writing process, known as 'analeptic thought' or casting your mind back in time, proved to be inspirational. The 1961 paperback edition of *The White Goddess* became an instant hit with the new counterculture and was a work that had already inspired the teenage Dylan. It is a book that T S Eliot described as 'monstrous, stupefying, indescribable', but for a generation looking for something different it was, at the very least, the book to be seen with... even if not read. In 1963, Graves was poet as rock and roll star.

In an interview with *Rolling Stone* journalist Robert Shelton in 1966, however, Dylan was somewhat sneering about their meeting during the party at Tregunter Road:

'I met him in England. He talked to somebody while I was singing 'Hollis Brown' and I didn't even know who Robert Graves was. He got up and talked to four young guys, who call themselves "professionals". They sang in the Blue Angel, or something like that. One played the accordion, one played the string bass, and one played the Gretsch rhythm guitar and one played the slide trombone. And Robert Graves went over and talked to them to find out about music, while I was singing. So, I stopped singing and said who's that guy?'

Later, in his book *Chronicles*, Dylan admitted that he did know of Graves' work, describing a time before his visit to London: 'Invoking the poetic muse was something I didn't know about yet … In a few years' time, I would meet Robert Graves himself in London. We went for a brisk walk around Paddington Square. I wanted to ask him about some of the things in his book, but I couldn't remember much about it.'

> Between Number 9 and the Troubadour is Redcliffe Square, which is certainly large enough for a 'brisk walk'. Could Dylan have strolled with Robert Graves in the early hours of the morning after the Tregunter Road party, having discussions that would profoundly influence him?
>
> **Map ref. 15**

In 1963 there was no Paddington Square in London, although there is now. However, between Number 9 and the Troubadour is Redcliffe Square, which is certainly large enough for a 'brisk walk'. Could Dylan have strolled with Robert Graves in the early hours of the morning after the Tregunter Road party, having discussions that would profoundly influence him? The woman described in 'Visions of Johanna' and large parts of that classic Dylan track are said to be heavily influenced by *The White Goddess*.

After the party was over, Dylan met up with Hans Fried at Collett's Record and Book Shop in Charing Cross Road. Fried tells us that *The White Goddess* was very much on Dylan's mind and that their discussions in the shop centred around the work. No less an expert than Michael Gray, the original Dylanologist, says that the two men spent over three hours discussing the book at The Star, a Soho coffee shop.

It seems, then, that the young Dylan was somewhat in awe of this titan of literature. In Robert Graves did he see an inspirational figure who would lead him on his lifelong journey from folk singer to poet and artist? A journey that would culminate in his Nobel Prize for Literature in 2016? Although we have learned to take *Chronicles* with a large pinch of salt when it comes to accuracy, there seems to be more than enough evidence that the two men met at Tregunter Road in 1963 and went for a walk together nearby.

It's also plausible that Dylan abruptly cut off singing 'Ballad of Hollis Brown', one of his more poetic songs from the time, because of Robert Graves' interruption. The band that Graves was talking to was Los

Valldemosa, from the village of Deià in Majorca where the Graves family had set down roots many years before, and he knew them well. Los Valldemosa played a mixture of Spanish, Majorcan and Calypso music. They were spotted in Palma, Majorca and offered a contract at the Blue Angel club off Piccadilly. They were even interviewed by the BBC. Coincidentally, Graves' passing interest in folk music was the reason he had lent the money to start the Troubadour club; his son, William, suggests that it was the success of *The White Goddess* which allowed him to do so.

After the debauched few days of drug-induced sing-songs at Tregunter Road, the party ground to an abrupt halt. The butler finally made himself visible, rang Rory's father and had Farina and Von Schmidt and their party turfed out of the house.

By the tail end of the '60s, Lord McEwen finally had enough of partying folkies and the house was sold. It became the Thai Embassy, which it remains to this day.

In late January 1963, Dylan flew back to the USA, in many ways a transformed man. The immediate and practical implication of his London visit was that he would change the album already recorded, taking out some songs and adding in ones he had learned (or 'appropriated') in London. *The Freewheelin' Bob Dylan* is the real start of Dylan as poet and artistic magpie.

Commentators have seen this London experience as one of musical appropriation, but what if the artistic course of his life was changed after meeting Graves at Tregunter Road? What if the young Dylan now had a new idol, muse and mentor, replacing Woody Guthrie, folk singer and social archivist, with the poet and novelist and classicist Robert Graves?

> Commentators have seen this London experience as one of musical appropriation, but what if the artistic course of his life was changed after meeting Graves at Tregunter Road?
>
> **Map ref. 16**

There is further evidence that their encounter stayed with Dylan. Ross Altman from the magazine *Folkworks* suggests that in January 1964, exactly a year after the Tregunter Road party, Dylan, in an echo of his death bed trip to Woody Guthrie, went to visit Robert Graves at his home in Deià, Majorca. An obituary for Graves had mistakenly been published, and although he would live for many years more, many fans were now making a pilgrimage to see him.

Dylan, then famous, flew to Deià, a copy of his album *The Times They Are A-Changin'* under his arm. Perhaps this title is not merely a comment on the political climate but rather a loaded reference to a Graves who Dylan might have felt couldn't understand how a mere folk singer could become a real poet? Did Dylan want to show Graves that the song he had interrupted during the party at Tregunter Road, 'Hollis Brown', was now recorded and critically acclaimed? An ill Graves refused to see Dylan, who returned to the USA and immediately set out on a road trip. He was in a creative rush like never before. David Hajdu, a friend of both Farina and Von Schmidt, has confirmed that Dylan was by then a writer with literary aspirations, seeing himself as more than a songwriter.

On Friday, April 12 1963, a few short months after his visit to Tregunter Road, Dylan gave one of his most significant concerts at Town Hall, New York. Significant not only for being the first performance on stage of a number of his most revered songs – including the poetic 'Boots of Spanish Leather' and the song aired at Tregunter Road, 'Don't Think Twice It's Alright' – but because he used this occasion to say farewell to Woody Guthrie, his first muse. Guthrie would live until 1967, but as Dylan stood on the stage with his 'tousled hair and hobo clothes he looked as he'd looked when he first entered New York ... a living breathing singing Woody Guthrie junior' – as it notes on the sleeve of *The Bootleg Series Volumes 1–3*. He finished the concert with 'Last Thoughts on Woody Guthrie'. But this time he doesn't sing. For the first and only time he gave his farewell in a poem.

Years later, Dylan was still trying to court the attention of Robert Graves. When Colombia needed a Spanish translation for an album cover, Dylan specifically asked that they approach Graves. Again, Graves declined.

There is one more clue that this briefest of meetings has stayed with Dylan. On the official Bob Dylan website (bobdylan.com), there is a page of suggested reading: Dylan's own books, as well as books about Dylan and the works of his poetic and singing contemporaries. At the very end is one suggestion that looks somewhat out of place, from a different time, of a very different style: *The White Goddess*.

Chapter 3
THE MAY FAIR

In 1962, Philip Saville, a British director of TV drama, heard Bob Dylan sing in a Greenwich Village club called Pastor's Place, while on a visit to New York – and was impressed. A couple of years later, when he was looking to cast an 'anarchic young student who wrote songs' for a BBC play, he thought Dylan might be the perfect fit.

Saville agreed with Albert Grossman, Dylan's manager, to pay a fee of $2000 (£500) plus the air fare to London, and accommodation at the May Fair hotel. (This already substantial fee, £11,000 in today's values, ended up being doubled, and the price of the flight home added on, when a technician's strike led to a delay in the recording of the play.) This is how the relatively unknown Bob Dylan ended up staying at the prestigious and expensive May Fair in December 1962.

The May Fair stands on Stratton Street, off Piccadilly, in London's West End. Often referred to incorrectly as the Mayfair, the hotel's name reveals something of the history of the area.

Mayfair was originally swampland around the river Tyburn. It got its name in 1686, when James II gave permission for a fair to be held during the first two weeks of May. The site of the historic fair is now Shepherd Market, a charming small square and piazza developed between 1735 and 1746 by Edward Shepherd.

For the two weeks in May, rich and poor alike thronged to see cattle auctions, watch plays, and drink. It was both popular and riotous, but as the area became gentrified the fair declined until it eventually ceased in 1764.

The former fields were turned into the new mansions and green squares of Mayfair. Wealthy families relocated westwards, and of the initial 227 houses built, 117 had titled owners. Mayfair became London's most desirable address. The district that had grown up on the site of the raucous fair retained its name, though not its reputation.

In the 19th century, 'new money' from industry and finance entered the area, looking for the prestige of the postcode but also wanting bigger and better houses to display their wealth. The 18th-century houses were pulled down or knocked together, and the décor became more ostentatious.

The First World War and the subsequent Great Depression depleted the coffers of Mayfair residents, forcing them to downsize and manage without their previous numbers of staff. Many of Mayfair's residential properties were demolished during this period, to be replaced by offices, modern apartment buildings and hotels, including the May Fair.

The May Fair hotel was opened by George V and Queen Mary in 1927. It soon became established as one of the most stylish hotels in Europe, hosting decadent parties and attracting extravagant displays of wealth. What's more, Bert Ambrose & His Orchestra played nightly for the guests, including royalty, who gathered to dance and dine.

During the Second World War, the May Fair was an oasis for guests who wanted to forget the horrors of the outside world. Jack Jackson and Harry Roy led the band as they entertained revellers in the lower ballroom, which – being in the basement – was safer. Life at the May Fair continued almost as if there was no war.

In the 1950s, the Danziger brothers, prolific film producers, bought the hotel and turned it once more into a magnet for the rich and famous.

In 1960, the hotel opened the Beachcomber restaurant. Resembling a film set, with waterfalls and pools and caiman crocodiles, it soon became known as the Crocodile Bar. Lighting effects could change the atmosphere from sunshine to thunder and lightning, even rainbows. It was a piece of theatre in which a fake pirate wandered about with a real parrot on his shoulder, and diners were serenaded by Polynesian music and enticed onto the dance floor by hula dancers.

By the 1960s, the May Fair had become the London home for show business royalty. A private cinema and a theatre were added as part of a revamp, and pianos were placed in every suite to cater for the needs of the many musicians and their entourages who came to stay.

Almost as soon as Dylan set foot in the May Fair, he knew it wasn't for him. As he explained in an interview with Robert Shelton, he disliked the stream of staff taking his bags from outside to inside, from lobby to lift, from lift to room – ending up, he complained, with about ten people each requiring tipping! He was also uncomfortable with what he described as the 'hooded little guards that looked like George Washington dressed up' who stood outside and, he felt, looked him over disapprovingly.

Dylan told Saville that the May Fair had a catalogue of complaints about him, including being unhappy with his appearance, his not wearing a tie, playing his guitar in the foyer, staying up all night and bringing in groupie girls off the streets. He was not yet famous enough for this to be tolerated, and shortly afterwards the BBC moved him to the Cumberland.

Map ref. 6

about him, including being unhappy with his appearance, his not wearing a tie, playing his guitar in the foyer, staying up all night and bringing in groupie girls off the streets. He was not yet famous enough for this to be tolerated, and shortly afterwards the BBC moved him to the Cumberland.

The Cumberland opened in December 1933, claiming to be Europe's largest hotel and containing 1000 guest rooms, each with its own hallway, bath and toilet. A big selling point was that guests could regulate the temperature of their rooms simply by moving a small valve lever, thereby recreating their home climate, 'be they from Alaska or Timbuctoo' as the publicity of the day said.

Located opposite Marble Arch, at the top of Oxford Street, the Cumberland is probably best known for being listed as the 'usual address' on the death certificate of Jimi Hendrix, who took a suite there in 1970, about two weeks before he died. Fittingly it was rebranded in 2019 as a Hard Rock hotel. Now filled with rock memorabilia, the property pays tribute to its former guests, including Dylan and Buddy Holly.

For the rest of his visit until he returned to America at the end of January 1963, Dylan stayed at the Cumberland or with various friends and acquaintances he met along the way, in particular at 9 Tregunter Road in west London, and at Saville's Hampstead home, where he regaled the Spanish au pairs with his songs.

Saville returned home one evening to find Dylan serenading the young women with a song so beautiful that he decided it must be in the BBC play he was producing for the BBC. That song was 'Blowin' in the Wind'.

The play, set in an English boarding house, was *Madhouse on Castle Street*, written by Evan Jones. One of the lodgers locks himself in his room, leaving a note stating that he has decided to retire from the world until the world has changed. Rehearsals began and it soon transpired that Dylan was finding it impossible to deliver his spoken lines. A solution was found by splitting his part in the play into two roles and bringing in a professional actor, David Warner, for the part with more speaking, leaving Dylan to concentrate on singing. In the end, he spoke just one line: 'Well, I don't know, I'll have to go home and think about it.' As much as Dylan appears to have been drawn to the idea of acting throughout his career, it has proved to be a challenge for him on more than one occasion, and poor reviews have littered his efforts.

Saville later remarked that Dylan's substantial fee was the most money ever paid for a singer to provide the opening and closing music for a play and deliver only one spoken line! It's impossible to say how well Dylan did because the BBC destroyed its copies of the play, and nothing remains apart from a couple of extremely rare recordings made at the time by viewers. The recordings reveal Dylan singing four songs: 'Blowin' in the Wind', which opened the play; 'The Ballad Of The

Gliding Swan', composed by Evan Jones and rewritten by Dylan; and two American traditional songs, 'Hang Me, Oh Hang Me', and 'Cuckoo Bird'.

In 1964 Dylan returned to London for a concert at the Royal Festival Hall on 17 May. Once more he stayed at the May Fair, perhaps accustomed by then to the trappings of wealth. The concert was a big success, and when it was over an old school fried, John Bucklen, went backstage to say hello. Dylan was happy to see him, even proudly showing him a telegraph from John Lennon saying he was sorry he couldn't make it to the show. Bucklen could hardly reconcile the performer on stage now being lauded by the Beatles with the Bob Zimmerman he had known at school.

After a night travelling round London to drop in on parties and acquaintances, the two old friends made it back to the May Fair with a couple of girls. Dylan argued with hotel staff, who wanted to stop him taking his girl up to his room, but when Bucklen suggested they went elsewhere Dylan pointedly told him not to interfere. Bucklen left, and was not to see his old friend again for over 20 years, when Dylan apologised for his behaviour in London, saying he'd been under a lot of pressure.

Dylan checked out of the May Fair after the Royal Festival Hall concert, taking some headed notepaper from the hotel in his bag. He'd already written one song on that paper during his week in London, which he performed at the Festival Hall. That song was 'It Ain't Me, Babe'. A facsimile of the notepaper and its lyrics can be seen in *The Bob Dylan Scrapbook*, a collection of memorabilia and stories illustrating his life from 1956 to 1966.

After checking out, he headed for a holiday in Greece with a couple of friends, travelling by car via France, where they met up with the singer Nico. She joined Dylan as they headed to Athens, also fitting in a trip to the Berlin Wall.

This was a hugely creative period for Dylan, and the May Fair notepaper came in handy to write down the stream of song lyrics as they came to his mind. Some of the songs were destined for his next album, *Another Side of Bob Dylan*. They included a trio of songs reflecting on his relationship with his girlfriend Suze: 'Ballad in Plain D', 'To Ramona', and 'Mama, You Been on My Mind'. Sadly, the latter, a beautiful love song, was one that Dylan rejected from the final album listing.

Dylan's third stay at the May Fair was in 1966, by which time he was world-famous. The 1966 tour – taking in Australia as well as some European countries – is one of the legendary tours of popular music history. No longer alone for the entire set, Dylan now had a backing band – later to be known as The Band, but then called the Hawks from their time playing with Ronnie Hawkins. Robbie Robertson, guitarist with the Hawks, to whom Dylan offered the job of lead guitarist on the tour, persuaded Dylan to take all of the Hawks with him. Only drummer Levon Helm declined the invitation, to be replaced by Mickey Jones.

Dylan's 'electric' tour unleashed a storm of controversy. Everyone had something to say, be it praise or loathing. Dylan resolutely stood by his decision to play the second half of his set with the Hawks, ignoring everyone who said he should have left them at home. It was during this tour that a member of the audience at Manchester Free Trade Hall famously shouted 'Judas' at Dylan – but by then members of the audience at each and every date he played had accused him of being a traitor.

Whatever anyone's opinion of his music, Dylan was pushing himself to his limit. It is a matter of conjecture as to what substances may have been helping him to keep going, but there's no doubt that he was exhausted, both physically and mentally. Robbie Robertson kept a watchful eye on him, worrying that the tiny amount he was eating at the time was not enough to sustain him through the demands of his concerts. Somehow Dylan continued, but his poor physical state can be seen in the photographs and videos of the time.

Photographs taken at a press conference at the hotel on 3 May 1966 by Fiona Adams show a thoroughly bored and fed-up Dylan. Adams recalls that Dylan's dislike of the proceedings led him at one point to climb out of a window and onto the balcony overlooking Berkeley Street.

We can work out where the photographs that day were taken because in some of them it's possible to make out the sign for the Stratstone Garage, which is still open for business on the opposite side of the road.

As in his 1964 visit to London, Dylan was lauded by the biggest stars of the time. There was a stream of visitors to the May Fair, including a jittery Johnny Cash, who was so keen that his wife should not know where he was that he hid in a wardrobe, presumably fearing her disapproval, when there was a knock at the door. He and Dylan played country tunes together, but only once he was sure he was not going to be discovered.

The Beatles called by to play him *Revolver*, their latest album. Dylan suggested that they wrote each other a song to record, but made it clear he didn't want a 'Please Please Me' type number. In a wry exchange, Dylan asked the Beatles if girls were still screaming for them, adding that he was certainly attracting screaming himself, but maybe not for the same reason.

Later that evening Dylan and John Lennon were filmed taking a trip in a limousine by D A Pennebaker, who was part of Dylan's entourage and filming the 1966 European tour. Dylan was clearly feeling ill and could barely speak, and the driver was asked to go slowly. The resulting film footage shows Lennon looking uncomfortable, and keeping a very straight face as he doled out the Englishman's perennial piece of advice: 'Pull yourself together'!

Lennon and the other Beatles came to Dylan's final concert of the tour at the Royal Albert Hall. They decided to visit Dylan at the May Fair after the concert, perhaps feeling he might need cheering up after the mixed reception he'd received, but Dylan was in no fit state to see visitors.

He had returned to the hotel worn out and close to collapse. Albert Grossman called Robbie Robertson down to Dylan's suite and asked him to help: Dylan had more or less passed out sitting in a chair. Grossman suggested that Robertson run Dylan a bath, hoping it might revive him enough to receive the waiting visitors. Dylan was delirious, and much too far gone for a simple soak to sort him out. At one point, Robertson popped out of the bathroom after hearing a knock at the door. When he went back in, he saw that Dylan had sunk into the water, and was almost drowning.

The Beatles were at the door but they were turned away while Robertson got Bob out of the bath, wrapped him in a big towel and put him to bed. Then, while Dylan slept, Robertson went off to party the night away. The next day a revived Dylan headed home to New York.

Chapter 4
THE SAVOY

The Savoy is the London hotel with which Bob Dylan is usually associated, largely because much of the time he spent there in 1965 was recorded in D A Pennebaker's film *Dont Look Back*.

The Savoy opened in 1889. Located between one of London's central arteries, the Strand, and the river Thames, it was built by Richard D'Oyly Carte, the theatrical impresario. Its location was one of the things that made the Savoy so special, and the hotel made the most of it: balconies designed by the architect and designer A H Mackmurdo allowed guests to dine outside

> The Savoy is the London hotel with which Bob Dylan is usually associated, largely because much of the time he spent there in 1965 was recorded in D A Pennebaker's film *Dont Look Back*.
>
> **Map ref. 7**

while overlooking the Thames. Inside, the designers created a classically Victorian décor with an emphasis on luxury and comfort.

Six months after the hotel opened, Auguste Escoffier, known as the 'king of chefs and chef of kings', was brought in by hotel manager César Ritz to reverse falling profits. Escoffier only spoke French, and was fond of saying that if he learned English he might start to cook like them. His most famous creation, for Dame Nellie Melba, was Peach Melba served in a swan carved out of ice. Escoffier's (and Ritz's) reign ended ignominiously when he was discovered to have taken substantial bribes from food suppliers.

By the time Richard D'Oyly Carte died in 1901, a block of land adjacent to the hotel had been acquired. Rupert D'Oyly Carte, Richard's son, was then Chairman of the Board. The site was levelled in 1903 and architect Thomas Collcutt designed the new blocks so that the hotel entrance now faced forward, onto the Strand but set back from it. Access is via Savoy Court, the only road in the UK where it is obligatory to drive on the right-hand side.

For the new century, in came light, bright Edwardian design, thanks to a fashionable revival of 18th-century, Robert Adam-style interiors, replacing the darker Victorian design throughout the hotel.

In 1910 the river-facing balconies were removed, allowing the rooms to be extended, and to make way for more bathrooms. In 1889 there were 67 bathrooms between 200 guest rooms. Guests had the option of having the nearest adjacent bathroom configured into their suite as a private bathroom, or the cheaper alternative of sharing a bathroom. All rooms were en suite after the reconfiguration.

In the same decade, the central courtyard was built over and became the Lancaster Ballroom. The interior of the ballroom was designed by French architect René Sergent and survives to the present day.

In the 1920s, the hotel embraced the Art Deco style, most notably with the iconic 'Savoy' sign created by architect Howard Robertson in stainless steel and spanning the entire width of Savoy Court. Robertson, later Sir Howard Robertson, continued to design Art Deco interiors for the Savoy until the 1950s, and though the hotel flirted in the second half of the 20th century with more modern design, it returned to the Art Deco and Edwardian styles in its four-year long refurbishment between 2007 and 2011.

The Savoy was the first hotel in Britain to introduce electricity, lifts, hot and cold running water, 24-hour room service and a fine dining restaurant – all unimaginable luxuries at the start of the 20th century. It's worth remembering that prior to the 20th century it was generally considered wise only ever to sleep in your own bed, or in the homes of friends and family. Poor mattresses and horrible food were what most people could expect from staying in a hotel. When the Savoy first opened, it offered the rich somewhere like home to stay.

Jazz music also helped make the Savoy a destination for new generation. In the UK, jazz – its rhythms first played by black African American musicians in New Orleans – had been popularised by white men in dinner suits. In the 1920s, the Savoy Havana Band and Savoy Orpheans played the hottest music in town. Dance music from the Savoy was broadcast on BBC radio throughout the '20s and '30s, and soon every notable hotel wanted its own jazz band.

Another important part of the hotel that attracted visitors from the day it opened its doors in 1889 was the American Bar. Its most famous employee was Harry Craddock, an English bar tender who had emigrated to America but returned to the UK in 1920 following Prohibition. During his spell at the bar he wrote *The Savoy Cocktail Book* featuring his creations, including the White Lady and Corpse Reviver #2. Published in 1930, it remains in print today.

On 26 April 1965 Dylan flew into Heathrow for his first tour of Great Britain. He was booked into Room 208 of the Savoy, a suite overlooking the river and costing £70 per week (about £1,450 in today's values, a figure that fails to convey the true cost today, when a suite at the Savoy can cost as much as £6,000 for a single day). When a *Daily Mail* reporter asked why he was staying at a hotel where even minor clerks wore swallow-tailed jackets, Dylan retorted that he couldn't live in a shack. The choice of the Savoy spoke volumes about Dylan's increasing fame and success, even if he himself was insisting that he didn't think of himself as a star and believed that in a couple of years he'd be back where he started.

Among Dylan's party were his old friend Bob Neuwirth, his manager Albert Grossman, film-maker D A Pennebaker and the film crew, and his erstwhile lover, Joan Baez. They were joined on 7 May by the poet Allen Ginsburg, who flew in from Prague, and – after the tour was over – by Sara Lownds, who was to become Sara Dylan later that year. Sara had put Pennebaker in touch with Grossman, who was married to a friend of hers, while she was working for a film company.

Joan Baez, though invited to be part of Dylan's entourage, soon understood that she and Dylan had different expectations of her purpose on the trip. Baez assumed she'd be invited on stage with Dylan, to be introduced to British audiences as she had introduced Dylan to her audiences in the USA. Unfortunately for Baez, Dylan had no intention of sharing the limelight. As he said: 'I can fit into her music, but she doesn't fit into my music – my show. It would have been dumb.'

On 4 May, a jam session took place in Dylan's suite. Dylan sang ten songs, mostly traditional, with Baez accompanying him on a number of them. They include the pair singing the beautiful Irish/Scottish folk song 'The Wild Mountain Thyme', a small portion of which can be seen in *Dont Look Back*. The unedited original was released in 2015 on the *Collector's Edition* of *The Best of the Cutting Edge 1965–1966: The Bootleg Series, Vol 12*, which was limited to 5,000 copies.

In *Dont Look Back* (the spelling, without an apostrophe, was Pennebaker's decision), some of the scenes featuring Baez can make for painful watching. She has written about how unhappy she felt at losing what she saw as her 'special relationship' with Dylan. On 5 May, she wrote to her sister Mimi that Dylan had become 'unbelievably unmanageable' and that she couldn't stand to be around him. Baez gave Mimi a list of some of the things she was finding unbearable, including that Dylan was walking around with a cane, had tantrums, ordered fish (why this was upsetting is not clear), got drunk, and stopped off every morning to buy all the newspapers that might have his name in them.

Eventually, Baez left the tour.

Friends and admirers came in droves to pay court to Dylan, and his suite at the Savoy was always full of people. The Beatles and the Rolling Stones popped by, as well as the Animals and the Pretty Things and Nico, his friend from his trip to Greece in 1964. Manfred Mann dropped in to give Dylan a copy of their cover version of his song 'With God on our Side'. Other visitors included folk singers Martin Carthy and Dorris Henderson, guitarist John Renbourn, and music publicist Anthea Joseph (whom Dylan had been told to ask for at the Troubadour when he first arrived in London). Sometimes, Dylan detached from the crowd as if retreating into an internal world. Bashing out lyrics on his black Remington typewriter, he seemed oblivious to the activity around him.

The Beatles had been captivated by *The Freewheelin' Bob Dylan*, finding it an original and wonderful album, and playing the disc until they wore it out. In advance of the 1965 tour they had been quoted in the press saying that they admired Dylan, and the *Melody Maker* headline of 9 January ran: 'Beatles say – Dylan shows the way'. That headline may have been responsible for kicking off Dylan mania. Dylan himself said of the tour that the fans' reaction to him was unlike anything he'd ever experienced before. The Beatles cannily remained out of shot in Pennebaker's film, but they visited on more than one occasion and came to see Dylan at one of his London concerts.

Dont Look Back is remembered by many as much for the scenes in the Savoy involving Scottish folk singer Donovan as for Bob Dylan himself.

In 1965, Donovan's star was rising. He had been voted 'Brightest Hope' by readers of the *New Musical Express*. When Dylan came to London, the press had a field day, comparing the two singers and asking whether Donovan was the English Dylan. Interviewers asked Dylan what he thought of Donovan. For his part, Dylan was interested enough to have listened a few times to Donovan's song 'Catch the Wind', and to have talked about him with Allen Ginsberg. He invited Donovan round to the Savoy one afternoon.

Donovan came to Dylan's suite with a few of his friends. Earlier in the day, Dylan had been at a function where masks were handed out, and he thought it would be funny to put them on for Donovan's arrival. If this was intended to throw the younger singer off his stride, it failed: Donovan just sat down and chatted away until the masks were gradually removed. Dylan was the last to remove his. The scene with the masks, recounted by Donovan in his autobiography, did not make it into *Dont Look Back*.

The next part of Donovan's meeting with Dylan is also not seen in the film. The pair exchanged songs, as singers often do. There are different versions of the story in circulation, and Donovan himself is quiet on the subject.

The song Donovan offered first was a pastiche of Dylan's own 'Mr. Tambourine Man', in which he substituted the words 'golden tangerine eyes' for 'Mister Tambourine Man'. By all accounts, Dylan appears to have been gracious about being played a rendition of his own work. Donovan said that he'd heard it somewhere and assumed it was an old folk song, to which Dylan apparently replied that it was not an old folk song – yet. As a musician well known for borrowing from other sources, Dylan may well have found it amusing.

Pennebaker later recollected: 'Dylan was sitting there with this funny look on his face, listening to "Mr. Tambourine Man" with these really weird words, trying to keep a straight face. Then Dylan says, "Well, you know, that tune ... I have to admit that I haven't written all the tunes I'm credited with, but that happens to be one that I did write!" I'm sure Donovan never played the song again.'

Another version says that Donovan was upfront about having heard Dylan sing the song at the Royal Festival Hall in 1964, and said that he had gone home afterwards and written his own song based on what he remembered. Whatever exactly happened, Dylan refused to allow the episode to go into the film.

At one point during the party that was going on in the room, Dylan asked Derroll Adams if there were any poets like Allen Ginsberg around. Adams was an American banjo player and friend of folk singer Ramblin' Jack Elliot, both of whom influenced Donovan. Adams suggested Dominic Behan, but Dylan replied that he didn't want to hear 'anyone like that'. When another person, out of shot in the film, drunkenly responded that Dominic Behan was a friend of his, the atmosphere changed. Maybe to alleviate the tension, Donovan started strumming a tune on a guitar and began to sing one of his own compositions, 'To Sing for You'.

Dylan said to Adams, 'He sounds like Jack', and responded enthusiastically after the first verse – 'It's a good song!' – and then listened to the remainder in silence. As soon as Donovan finished, Dylan walked over to take the guitar, which Donovan released, albeit a little reluctantly. Dylan, removing the shades he habitually wore, played 'It's All Over Now, Baby Blue', grinning broadly. He followed that up with 'Love Minus Zero/No Limit'.

Donovan visited Dylan's suite at the Savoy on a few more occasions. One time he joined Joan Baez in writing out the cue cards that would be used in the filming of Dylan's song 'Subterranean Homesick Blues', at nearby Savoy Steps.

Notions of a rivalry between the two singers were laid to rest on 8 May, when *Melody Maker* ran a headline 'Dylan Digs Donovan'.

When he called to the hotel shortly before Dylan returned to the USA, Donovan was led by Bob Neuwirth through a silent apartment to a door that opened into a small room, and told that Bob was inside. It was a TV room, illuminated only by the television itself. Donovan went in and sat on the floor, noticing Dylan sitting in a big, soft chair. As his eyes grew accustomed to the light, he realised he wasn't alone, then, as he wrote later, an unmistakeable voice piped up, 'Hello Donovan, hawareya?'. It was John Lennon. Paul, George and Ringo were also there and watching, improbable though it sounds, ice skating. Later, he got a lift home with George Harrison, in one of four custom-designed Minis lined up outside the Savoy.

Donovan has stated in his autobiography how he believes he compares with Dylan: 'His lyrics are without equal in all of popular music but I think that musically I am the more creative and influential.'

Another frequent visitor to Dylan's suite at the Savoy was Marianne Faithfull, a singer whose star was in the ascendant after her hit with the Stones' song 'As Tears Go By'. The 18-year-old was in the early stages of pregnancy when she came to the Savoy. In her own words, she worshipped Dylan but was engaged to be married to a student called John Dunbar. At the Savoy she observed the 'egos all playing off each other at the Court of King Bob', with Dylan as the 'mercurial, bemused centre of the storm, almost waiflike and vulnerable'.

Faithfull was attracted to Dylan, loving his 'proto punk hair, black leather, Spanish boots, and druggy shades', but above all she liked the talk – all that 'cerebral jangling'. When she heard that he was writing a song about her, she realised that she had been elevated to 'Chief Prospective Consort', a role she knew she would have to decline.

When the scene was finally set for her seduction, she told Dylan that she was pregnant and engaged to be married. He ripped up the paper in his typewriter, leaving her to wonder ever afterwards what lyrics she may have inspired.

The night before his first Royal Albert Hall concert on 9 May, Dylan held an impromptu party at the Savoy. His suite was packed with friends and admirers when a member of the hotel staff entered to say that glass had been thrown out of one of the windows. Guest Anthea Joseph's recollection is that two people had locked themselves in the bathroom and started chucking the beautiful 1930s' glass shelves through the window.

Dylan was enraged. He loudly rounded on everyone in the suite, asking who was responsible. The scene continued for some time, Dylan angrily saying that he would not be responsible for the behaviour of people he didn't even know. Maybe the toll of being – in Joseph's words – 'over-peopled' came to the boil. It never became clear who threw the glass. Dylan finally calmed down, and suggested to everyone present: 'Be groovy or leave!'

Dylan stayed on at the Savoy for two more weeks after his eight-date tour ended on 10 May. You have to wonder about the bill for damages, and whether the entire suite had to be repainted after all the smoking.

Dont Look Back was released a full two years after the events it captured on camera, and despite Dylan's initial insistence that many changes would have to be made, in the end he agreed to the first version Pennebaker showed him. Perhaps it was already the past – and holding onto the past is something Dylan has never done.

Chapter 5
SAVOY STEPS

Savoy Steps is a cobbled alley behind the Strand, a major road in the heart of London's West End. Actual steps had linked the alley to the Strand for centuries, but despite the name you'll not find any today; they were demolished to make way for a new building in 1923. You can see what they looked like thanks to the drawings of artist Alan Stapleton, who drew many of London's alleys and byways, publishing a collection in the same year the steps were destroyed.

Along one side of Savoy Steps is the Queen's Chapel of the Savoy, an extraordinarily beautiful church dating back to the 16th century. In his later years, Henry VII worried that he had not done enough good deeds to earn a place in heaven, and ordered that a hospital for the poor be built on the site of the then derelict Savoy Palace. The chapel is all that remains of the hospital's extensive buildings.

By way of coincidence, the English folk singer Martin Carthy, Dylan's friend from his first visit to London in 1962, had been a chorister at that very chapel as a child. To this day, the Chapel's choir, formed of six professional male singers and up to 21 boys from St Olave's school in Kent, sing much of the service during term time. The Queen's Chapel is a Royal Peculiar: it is subject to the direct jurisdiction of the monarch, and its Sunday services begin with the national anthem.

On the other side of Savoy Steps is the four-storey rear extension to Norman House, which fronts onto the Strand. Norman House is architecturally a bit of a mess – or, as the planners say, it has an 'unresolved' skyline. The building was originally well-balanced, but later re-development of the Strand led to it lose a wing and thus its symmetry. Its construction led to the removal of the steps leading to the Strand. Today the part of Norman House bordering Savoy Steps houses the laundry rooms and technical services department for the hotel. It is called the School Block because it stands on the site of a school which formerly provided choristers for the Chapel.

On 8 May 1965, Bob Dylan stood on the corner of Savoy Steps where the Queen's Chapel meets Savoy Hill, to be filmed by D A Pennebaker. On that day the School Block was covered in scaffolding, and builders' materials were piled on the pavement, but apart from that the alley is the same today. A planning application to Westminster Council from the owner of the land, the

Duchy of Lancaster, to demolish and rebuild Norman House was approved in 2018 and, at the time of writing, scaffolding once again covered the buildings.

Dylan had suggested to Pennebaker that he wanted to make a film to accompany his song 'Subterranean Homesick Blues'. He'd recorded the track in New York earlier that year and it opened the first, electric, side of his new album, *Bringing It All Back Home*. By the end of May 1965, that album would reach Number 1 in the UK album charts. Also in the charts that year were three of his previous albums: *The Freewheelin' Bob Dylan*, *The Times They Are A-Changin'* and *Another Side of Bob Dylan*. Two singles, 'Subterranean Homesick Blues' and 'The Times They Are A-Changin'', had both reached Number 9 in the UK singles chart. By contrast, 'Subterranean Homesick Blues' only just scraped into the Top 40 in the USA. Perhaps British audiences were readier to accept Dylan's new musical direction.

On first hearing 'Subterranean Homesick Blues', John Lennon is quoted as saying he didn't know how he would ever compete. 'You don't have to hear what Bob Dylan says, you just have to hear how he says it', he explained. Lennon later produced Harry Nilsson's 1974 garage rock-style cover of the song, featuring Ringo Starr on drums.

Dylan's idea was to flip cue cards inscribed with key words and phrases to accompany the song. In the 1960s there was no 'music video' as such. However, Scopitone had been invented and was being manufactured in France. This was a piece of jukebox-like technology that played a three-minute film clip to accompany a 45-inch single, and by the early '60s was popular in the USA. It was partly to make a Scopitone clip that Pennebaker was filming Dylan that day.

The day of 8 May was officially a break from Dylan's acoustic tour of the United Kingdom, which had begun on 30 April. He had already played six concerts in six cities. On the following two nights, he would conclude the tour in London's Royal Albert Hall.

There were three choices of location for the shoot, and Savoy Steps was the second one to be tried. Pennebaker's first attempt was made in Embankment Gardens, a small park situated between the Savoy and the river Thames. In this shoot, Dylan flips the cue cards while in the background, to his right, the Beat poet Allen Ginsberg, a friend of Pennebaker's, and Dylan's friend and tour manager Bob Neuwirth are having a conversation. For some reason Ginsberg spends a lot of time removing his jumper.

Ginsberg had been deported from Prague, and arrived in London the day before filming for 'Subterranean Homesick Blues' began. He was due to perform at a Beat Generation poetry reading in the Royal Albert Hall on 11 June.

This was not the first deportation that year for Ginsberg. In February he had been deported from

Cuba. He later suggested that this was in response to his comments about the sex appeal of Che Guevara or his call for the legalisation of marijuana. The blockade on flights between the USA and Cuba meant that his deportation involved a stopover in Prague.

When Ginsberg arrived in Prague, he stayed with friends. He must have made a considerable impression in the city, because 100,000 people voted him 'King of May' that year, an honorary title bestowed under a recently revived folk custom that was tolerated by the normally repressive authorities as part of the May Day festival. Wearing his paper crown, Ginsberg joined a parade through Prague, preaching revolution. The authorities were not impressed, and a week later he was deported. Rather touchingly, an Allen Ginsberg Freedom Festival would be organised by the Czech Republic in 2015, to commemorate that week's events.

On the plane from Prague to London, Ginsberg wrote a poem about the events containing the lines:

And tho' I am the King of May, the Marxists have
    beat me upon the street,
kept me up all night in Police Station, followed
    me thru Springtime
Prague, detained me in secret and deported me
    from our kingdom by airplane.

When Ginsberg joined Dylan and Neuwirth for the filming, Embankment Gardens were in flower. In the film footage is a sign propped on an easel, announcing

Display of Paintings, with the paintings in and among the flower beds.

Unfortunately, filming in the gardens was interrupted by a policeman hitting Pennebaker on the shoulder as he was shooting, presumably because his activities made it more difficult for people to enjoy the gardens and the art on display.

Later that day there would be a third shoot on the roof of the Savoy with the rooftops of London in the background. By then the mild spring day had turned windy and Dylan, wearing an overcoat, had a battle to control the cue cards. Some were blown away and showered down onto the streets. In the rooftop clip, Neuwirth appears again, this time leaning on a cane, talking to Tom Wilson, record producer for Dylan (as well as for Frank Zappa and the Velvet Underground). Wilson is wearing a double-breasted coat, round glasses and a fez. The films from Embankment Gardens and the hotel rooftop were not seen until Martin Scorsese's 2005 film *No Direction Home*.

> The films from Embankment Gardens and the hotel rooftop were not seen until Martin Scorsese's 2005 film *No Direction Home*.
> **Map ref. 17**

But it was Savoy Steps that provided the location for what has gone down in history as the first ever music video. It opens with Dylan standing to the right of the picture as the music starts, holding a large pile of cards and looking directly at the camera. In the background Bob Neuwirth and Allen Ginsberg are again talking, animatedly, to one another. Ginsberg wears around his shoulders the jumper which he was busy removing in Embankment Gardens. Neuwirth and Ginsberg lean on walking canes as they speak – given Savoy Steps' proximity to a branch of Woolworths that used to be on the Strand, maybe they bought broom handles there for the purpose.

Dylan is wearing a shirt and a waistcoat. The weather, which had been dull for most of the week, was warming up. Dylan's role in the film was to fling down the pre-written cards, on each of which was a word or phrase from 'Subterranean Homesick Blues', roughly in sync with the track. The writing was on pieces of card used in the Savoy laundry to back freshly cleaned shirts. They were written by Dylan and some of his party at the Savoy, notably Joan Baez and Donovan. The occasional deliberate spelling mistake ('man whole', 'suckcess') and spellings

> But it was Savoy Steps that provided the location for what has gone down in history as the first ever music video. It opens with Dylan standing to the right of the picture as the music starts, holding a large pile of cards and looking directly at the camera.
>
> **Map ref. 8**

designed to highlight Dylan's accent ('pawking met-aws') added to the feeling of streetwise anarchy that the song generated.

Pennebaker filmed the entire track in one continuous take using his handheld camera. The use of cue cards hinted at black and white silent films, and the unexplained presence of Neuwirth and Ginsberg in the wings was more than a nod to slapstick comedy.

At the end of the film, as Ginsberg and Neuwirth stride away swinging their canes, Dylan walks off to the left, revealing for a brief moment a black car parked halfway down the alley. It's probably an Austin A40 Somerset, an 'everyman' car for the era, and probably not connected with the filming party.

The background of scaffolding and high walls, filmed in black and white with the camera held low to the ground, gave the film a gritty appearance. Many people assume it was shot in New York. In fact, the location could hardly be further from 'gritty', given that the Savoy Hotel, frequented by the wealthy and famous, is just a stone's throw away.

With its fast-paced, witty rhymes and vivid imagery, 'Subterranean Homesick Blues', in all of its 2 minutes and 22 seconds, is perfectly suited to Dylan's innovative visual accompaniment. Dylan himself has acknowledged the influence of Chuck Berry's 'Too Much Monkey Business' on the song, as well as what he has described as ''40s scat songs', where the singer imitates an instrument by ad-libbing nonsense syllables instead of lyrics. Others have added the Woody Guthrie song 'Take it Easy' (also known as 'Just Taking it Easy'), and the 'machine gun' couplets of the Beat poets to the list of influences

Pennebaker did not originally intend to use the 'Subterranean Homesick Blues' clip as the opening sequence for the film *Dont Look Back*. He planned to open the film with Dylan backstage intoning the words 'You start out standing' from 'She Belongs to Me', the song which includes the lines 'she don't look back'. In the end, he decided that a barely heard phrase sung by someone that the viewer might not know, and who had not been seen on stage at that point in the film, would not work.

As well as forming the introduction to *Dont Look Back*, Pennebaker also adapted 'Subterranean Homesick Blues' to be a trailer for the film. In the trailer, Dylan holds a card saying: 'Coming Soon'. It was an interesting choice of trailer in many ways. With Dylan knowingly looking straight into the camera as the clip begins, it served as an announcement that – far from the cinema verité that it appeared to be – the film was a performance.

Pennebaker's film clip cemented Dylan's image of '60s amphetamine cool and provided a literal portrayal of Dylan as street poet. But surely nobody could have foreseen quite how iconic those 2 minutes and

22 seconds would become and how many artists would imitate and develop the idea over the next half century. Among the more notable, Michael Hutchence of INXS used cue cards in the video to the band's track 'Mediate'. Actor Tim Robbins, in his role as a right-wing folk singer in the film *Bob Roberts*, flips through cards containing lyrics to his 'Wall Street Rap'. Even Pennebaker himself has parodied the cue card sequence in a short promotional film for the rock group The National made in 2010: he can be seen in the background leaning against a garage while members of the band flip through cards containing details of the broadcast.

It's not just bands and film-makers who have imitated the film. In 2012 the *Wall Street Journal* suggested that American visitors to the Olympic Games in London might like to visit Savoy Steps and be filmed making their own tribute to that spring day in 1965. Ordinary fans in their hundreds (including the authors of this book) have stood – and will continue to stand – where Dylan stood, re-enacting the clip with just a few pieces of paper and a marker pen. All that remains is to commemorate the site with a plaque for posterity.

TREGUNTER ROAD

SAVOY STEPS

CAMDEN

Legend
1. Flukes Cradle Cafe
2. Banner's Restaurant
3. Pindar of Wakefield
4. The King and Queen
5. Dobells Record Shop
6. The May Fair Hotel
7. Savoy Hotel
8. Savoy Steps
9. Royal Festival Hall
10. Royal Albert Hall
11. Queen's Gate Mews
12. Hammersmith Apollo
13. Earls Court Arena
14. The Troubadour
15. Redcliffe Gardens
16. Tregunter Road
17. Embankment Gardens

Paddington

Knightsbridg

Kensington

Hammersmith

Chelsea

Blackbushe 32 miles

BLACKBUSHE

FOLK CLUBS

SAVOY HOTEL

Chapter 6
ROYAL ALBERT HALL

The Royal Albert Hall is a world-famous concert hall in South Kensington. Its impressive neighbours include Kensington Gardens to the north and the Natural History Museum to the south.

In the space of 12 months in the mid-1960s, Bob Dylan was to give radically different performances in the venue, performances that led to his being included in artist Peter Blake's large triptych *Appearing At the Royal Albert Hall*, which can be seen on the wall by the café at Gate 12. You'll have to search quite hard to find him, but in the centre of the picture, surrounded by Bill Clinton, Dame Vera Lynn, Sir John Rutter, Iggy Pop, Stevie Wonder and the Royal Albert Hall's cat is the monochrome face of Bob Dylan.

Queen Victoria opened the Hall on 29 March 1871, following years of fallings out and changes of plan. The foundation stone she laid in 1867 is still there, underneath Block K of the stalls, Row 11, Seat 87. Beneath the stone is a cavity into which the Queen placed a time capsule containing gold and silver coins and an inscription by the Prime Minister. They have remained unseen ever since.

The Hall was built as a tribute to Victoria's husband, Prince Albert, who had died in 1861. At the opening ceremony the Queen said that she wished it to be called the Royal Albert Hall of Arts and Sciences instead of its intended name, the Central Hall of Arts and Sciences. The name stuck.

The Royal Albert Hall is constructed from warm red Aberdeen granite and bordered with a terracotta mosaic frieze paying tribute to human accomplishment throughout history. Its glass-domed roof was so distinctive that, during the Second World War, German bomber squads flying over London did not target it but instead used it as a navigation point.

The Hall's detractors tend to focus on its 'formless' shape, one commentator deriding it as a 'squat rotundity'.

The hall was originally planned to house flower shows and industrial exhibitions, and host meetings of scientific societies. Eventually it found its primary function as a concert hall. Unfortunately, major problems with its acoustics had to be addressed before the first concert could be performed. In fact, the echo in some parts of the auditorium remained so bad that a joke sprang up that concerts at the Albert Hall were good value for money because you could hear any piece played twice.

The problem with acoustics persisted over the years. Various solutions were tried, and by the time Bob Dylan first graced its stage in May 1965, a sound-reflecting canopy over the orchestra had been replaced with an aluminium inner dome in the roof to absorb the echo. In the late 1960s, 135 fibreglass sound-absorbing discs, known affectionately as 'mushrooms', would be suspended from the ceiling. In 2001, that number would be reduced to 85. In 2019, further improvements were made, and now the sound quality is the same no matter where a person sits in the hall.

By May 1965 Bob Dylan was a huge star. Four of his albums were in the Top 20 of the UK album charts, and 'Subterranean Homesick Blues' and 'The Times They Are A-Changin'' had reached the Top 10 in the singles charts. It was entirely appropriate that his UK tour should conclude with two dates in the prestigious Royal Albert Hall.

D A Pennebaker's iconic film *Dont Look Back* shows the build-up to the second of the two 1965 Royal Albert Hall dates, as well as some edited footage from the first concert. Pennebaker's film has been criticised for cutting short the concert performances, but the recordings were not lost. Many tracks can be heard on *Dont Look Back: The Outtakes*, a two-DVD bootleg from the film released in 2005.

Apart from spontaneous gigs in folk clubs on his first visit to London, Dylan's only previous concert in the UK had been at London's Royal Festival Hall in May 1964. This frequently overlooked show included the debut performance of 'Mr. Tambourine Man'. An album of the concert was finally released in Japan in 2015, but tracks are also available on a two-disc set entitled *Live 1962–1966: Rare Performances From The Copyright Collections*. This collection travels through Dylan's journey from ground-breaking acoustic folk artist to iconic force of pop culture.

Returning to tour the UK a year later, Dylan was booked to play the Royal Albert Hall, on 9 and 10 May 1965. The dates fell between the Boys Brigade's London Display and the Seventh Festival of Scotland In London.

> Dylan's debut performance of 'Mr. Tambourine Man' was at London's Royal Festival Hall in May 1964.
> **Map ref. 9**

In 1965 Bob Dylan's audience was a mixture of folk music fans, and young people who were drawn to his cool image and incredible songs. Dylan has said that his British audiences were the first to get what he was doing, as he transcended the labels of 'folk singer' and 'protest singer'.

Tickets for the Royal Albert Hall concerts had sold out in two hours when they were released, a couple of months earlier. One hundred and fifty tickets were held back for the first of the two dates for special guests, including the Beatles, Rolling Stones and Animals.

There was no set on the stage for his concert, just a tall stool and a couple of glasses of water. Dylan walked on wearing a black leather jacket, blue shirt buttoned to the top, black trousers and Cuban heeled boots, and carrying his acoustic guitar, a clutch of harmonicas and a harmonica rack. He opened the show with 'The Times They Are A-Changin''. The audience was spellbound, applauding tumultuously when the song finished.

On stage, Dylan was relaxed and in good humour, cracking the occasional joke. He announced the song 'It's Alright, Ma (I'm Only Bleeding)', adding 'ho, ho ho' with a grin, to the amusement of the audience. He got big laughs when he inserted some words into his song 'Talkin' World War III Blues' to refer to the folk singer Donovan hiding in his closet, a reference to the supposed rivalry between Dylan and the 'other folksinger'.

In the green room during the intermission following a rapturously received first half of the set, Dylan ventured to Bob Neuwirth that 'applause is bullshit'. Much as he enjoyed the adulation, he may have already sensed how quickly it could sour.

After his triumphant first date he left in the back of a chauffeur-driven car, sitting by the window into which young fans peered, keen for a glimpse of the star (an image to be recaptured the following year by photographer Barry Feinstein). Dylan remarked to his fellow passengers that there had been 'something special' about the concert. His manager, Albert Grossman, sitting next to Dylan, told him that the press was referring to him as an anarchist – because he didn't offer any solutions to the questions his songs asked. Dylan contrived to look slightly offended, but then asked mischievously if someone would 'give the anarchist a cigarette'.

His second date in 1965 was equally well received, but only one year later, the Royal Albert Hall was to witness a very different Dylan concert.

Well before May 1966, Dylan had metamorphosed into a new kind of star. The James Dean look was now gone. In its place were a couple of suits handmade by a tailor in Toronto, one in brown and black houndstooth, the other in salt and pepper tweed with leather piping on the jacket, complete with double-breasted waistcoat and drainpipe trousers. He also wore Beatle boots on his feet. When he wasn't on stage, he was rarely seen without his blue suede military jacket and custom Ray-Ban Wayfarer sunglasses. The hair was wilder than ever, and contrasted with the pallor of his skin.

His transition from folk singer to rock star had been gradual. Some would say that he made the transition via a stage of folk rock, but that's not a label Dylan recognised. Back in January 1965 he had recorded some of the tracks on *Bringing It All Back Home* with rock musicians, swapping his acoustic for an electric guitar. He explained that he was getting bored of his concerts, finding the audience response predictable. He was, he said, even thinking of quitting. *Bringing It All Back Home* alienated some of Dylan's folk purist fans, but it also broadened his fan base because Dylan had managed to fuse folk and rock in a way that proved extremely popular.

His appearance at the 1965 Newport Folk Festival, where he decided to play an electric set backed by the Butterfield Blues Band, cemented the direction of travel in no uncertain terms. What's more, his next album, *Highway 61 Revisited* – from which the single 'Like A Rolling Stone' was taken – was released in the UK in August 1965, and reached Number 4 in the charts.

So, by May 1966, when Dylan returned to the UK for another tour, there had already been plenty to warn his followers that this time would bring something new. His 1966 European tour again ended with two dates at the Royal Albert Hall, and now he was not alone. He had acquired a backing band, the Hawks, later to become The Band. In fact, only four Hawks came on the tour with Dylan: after 'going electric', Dylan received such negative reactions in the USA that drummer Levon Helm became so dispirited he decided not to subject himself to more of the same. Replacement drummer Mickey Jones sat in his place, alongside fellow Hawks Robbie Robertson, Garth Hudson, Rick Danko and Richard Manuel.

Before the two dates at the Royal Albert Hall, 27 and 28 May 1966, there had been booing and walk-outs from concert halls in eight British cities as well as during the concert played in Paris on the night of Dylan's birthday, 24 May. Reviews accused him of sacrificing lyric and melody to the 'God of big beat', and said that he had been 'buried in a grave of deafening drums'. As Mickey Jones said later, things were out of control. Here was somebody that everybody loved, but too many of his fans didn't like what he was doing – and they were showing their disapproval just as they had done in America.

During a to-become-legendary date on that UK tour, the reaction of one disgruntled member of the audience at the Free Trade Hall in Manchester was captured for posterity, as he shouted 'Judas' to Dylan. It's worth remembering that Dylan later said his own perspective on the booing was that you can kill someone with kindness too – another nod to the depth of his self-belief in the face of opposition.

Dylan didn't abandon his folk audience. Each night of his European concert tour consisted of two sets, the first entirely acoustic. Only in the second half did the Hawks came out to back him. Many of the audiences were perfectly happy with the acoustic first half, just wishing he'd left the band behind for the second.

In marked contrast to the good-natured banter of the previous year's dates, Dylan's interaction with the audience in 1966 was minimal, and frequently mocking. Before 'Just Like Tom Thumb's Blues', he declared to those wanting to know what happened to Woody Guthrie and Bob's 'protest songs': 'These are all protest songs – now come on! This isn't British music, it's American music.'

He told the audience that it wasn't true that he didn't like his old songs. He did like them, he insisted, but before launching in to 'I Don't Believe You', he said: 'It used to go like that, now it goes like this.'

The walkouts began in the second half. The mythology of the 1966 tour is that 'everyone' hated the electric sets, but that's clearly not true. Many stayed and appreciated the new direction Dylan was heading. But a large group of former fans were alienated and didn't hesitate to say so. This was all about their own feelings of betrayal, not the actual music.

Robbie Robertson – who was given the 1965 black Fender Telecaster played by Dylan in the electric set and subsequently used it himself right up until the mid '70s, including at Woodstock and the Isle of Wight Festival – appreciated Dylan sticking with the Hawks in the face of this hostility, but was equally bemused by the audience reaction. He knew the music was good.

Dylan's reaction, which can be seen and heard in the live recordings from the tour, was to supercharge the music with an energy that perhaps he took directly from the booing. He certainly never showed any sign of self-doubt. If anything, it firmed both his and the Hawks' resolve to play hard and loud. As Mickey Jones recalled: 'We kicked ass and took names.'

A film of the 1966 tour was released in 1972 as *Eat the Document*. Dylan, despite a complete lack of training, edited the footage himself, having dismissed the version by D A Pennebaker and Bob Neuwirth as too similar to *Dont Look Back*. An uneven and often criticised film, it was rejected by the original commissioners, TV company ABC, as incomprehensible, and has never been released on home video. Prints are rarely screened in cinemas.

Eat the Document none the less contains fascinating scenes, some of which reveal the diverse reactions to the 1966 tour. We hear comments of the nature that Dylan and his band were: trash/absolutely fantastic/overamplified/couldn't be heard/needed shooting. Some of the footage appears in Martin Scorcese's 2005 Dylan documentary, *No Direction Home*.

Another entertaining vignette that appears in that film shows Dylan reciting a monologue based on the signs on the wall outside a pet shop in Queensgate Mews, Knightsbridge. This frenetic and animated clip would years later form a highlight of *No Direction Home*. The pet shop is now derelict.

Reminiscent of the Dylan monologue filmed at Queensgate Mews is the first song recorded in 1967 for *The Basement Tapes* album, 'Tiny Montgomery'. It's a surreal, Edward Lear-like, cut-and-paste ramble, and lyrics such as Scratch Your Dad/Do That Bird/Suck That Pig/Pick That Drain/Flour That Smoke echo Dylan's gleeful playabout with words from the pet shop signs.

In charge of recording the 1966 sets at the Royal Albert Hall was sound engineer Richard Alderson. He had installed the sound system in the Gaslight club in New York in 1962, and was invited to record Bob Dylan playing there as a solo folk singer. A few years later, Albert Grossman asked him to build the sound system and record the 1966 tour. Incredibly, Alderson had very little idea of what was going to be required of him – he knew that Dylan had been playing electric but had no idea that the second half was going to be what it turned out to be.

> Another entertaining vignette that appears in that film shows Dylan reciting a monologue based on the signs on the wall outside a pet shop in Queensgate Mews, Knightsbridge. This frenetic and animated clip would years later form a highlight of *No Direction Home*.
>
> **Map ref. 11**

Alderson explained later that – in the absence of rehearsals or any kind of template for how to mike the electric band – he used one microphone for everyone and maybe two for Dylan. As a result, what was recorded was exactly what went out into the hall, all in one mix. His own theory was simple: if you put good microphones in front of good music, it will sound good.

On Grossman's advice, Alderson handed his tapes over to Dylan's record company, Columbia. It had sent expensive crews to record the shows, and preferred their recordings over Alderson's. For many years, Alderson didn't know if his tapes would ever become anything. They were finally released in 2016 as part of an epic, 36-CD box set, *The 1966 Live Recordings*. The concert from Manchester (Discs 19 and 20) had already been released in 1998 as part of *The Bootleg Series Vol. 4*. A concert from the boxset (London, 26 May 1966 – Discs 28 and 29) was released separately in November 2016 under the title *The Real Royal Albert Hall 1966 Concert*.

Can it be claimed that Bob Dylan was one of the original punk rockers? Citing his 1966 tour, culminating at the Royal Albert Hall, journalist and writer Steve Ricciutti has made this insightful assessment:

'It might be a stretch, but I think an argument can be made that the roots of punk go back much farther than the 70s in New York or London, and even back beyond the Stooges or MC5. Certainly the method in which Bob Dylan snarls his lyrics in a mix of love and contempt for his audience, deliberately altering the lyrical cadence, thumbing his nose at the fans that foolishly assume he's there merely to entertain them like a live jukebox, is behaviour that was mirrored later by Johnny Rotten and Joe Strummer. It's a part of rock and roll;

walking the razor's edge between art and entertainment, and it's what gives this genre an energy and urgency no other music can match.'

Despite joking as he left the Royal Albert Hall afterwards, surrounded by fans, that he wanted the names of everyone

> Despite joking as he left the Royal Albert Hall afterwards, surrounded by fans, that he wanted the names of everyone who booed him, Dylan was clearly exhausted.
>
> **Map ref. 10**

who booed him, Dylan was clearly exhausted. To some extent it seems he was able to feed off the negativity, but by the end of the tour he didn't want to go anywhere except home.

This was to be Bob Dylan's last appearance in the UK for 12 years. Grossman had set up a punishing schedule of dates that were to start after a short rest period, but in July '66 and soon after returning home, he had an accident on his motorbike. This put paid to all the plans and paved the way for a new Dylan to emerge, and a new creative period.

Dylan would return to the Royal Albert Hall only in 2013, and then again in 2015, after a near 50-year break with the venue. The reviews then were far kinder, indeed almost reverent.

Chapter 7
EARLS COURT AND BLACKBUSHE

Earls Court is a lively area in the Royal Borough of Kensington and Chelsea in West London. The District line of the London Underground links it to the more affluent parts of the borough – Fulham, South Kensington – but Earls Court is decidedly on the wrong side of the tracks.

In the 1960s and '70s, Earls Court became known as a bedsitter land after large Georgian houses were converted to bedsits, hotels and hostels, attracting global travellers, notably Australians, Kiwis and South Africans.

The Earls Court of this chapter, an important episode in the Bob Dylan story, is not the area but rather the Earls Court Exhibition Centre. The Exhibition Centre stood on the area's Warwick Road from 1937 until its demolition in 2014–2016. In 2020, the site is still awaiting development.

There had been a showground on the site opposite the Warwick Road exit of Earls Court station since 1887. An early attraction was Buffalo Bill Cody, who was part of the 'American Show'. Queen Victoria was one of many illustrious visitors.

The site's purpose as providing a home for shows and exhibitions was sealed for the 20th century with the construction of the Exhibition Centre. Work on the ambitious scheme began in 1935, and it had its grand opening with the Chocolate and Confectionery Exhibition on 1 September 1937. This display of joyous gluttony was to last for two years.

The building which housed the Exhibition Centre was an Art Moderne structure designed by American architect C Howard Crane, who had moved to London after the Great Depression. In the middle of the floor space was an enormous pool, which was used for watercraft exhibitions such as the Boat Show and covered with a retractable floor when not in use. The pool contained two and a quarter million gallons of water, and took four days both to fill and empty.

Over its 80-year history, the Earls Court Exhibition Centre was also a major London music venue, attracting artists from all over the world. At its height in the 1970s, let's not underestimate the amount of money it contributed to the local economy. It hosted the British

International Motor Show, the Ideal Home Show, the BRIT Awards and the Royal Tournament, and the list of acts to have appeared there is as impressive as any venue in musical history.

Slade and David Bowie were among the first rock acts to play the venue, and in 1975 Led Zeppelin played five nights that became the subject of books and films and the stuff of legend. One after-party gig was held at The Troubadour Club, just up the road, for a couple of hundred very privileged music fans.

After a 12-year absence from the UK, Bob Dylan came to play Earls Court in 1978. Back in 1966, as the crowds drifted away from the Royal Albert Hall after the last night of his infamous European 'electric' tour, no one could have believed it would be so long until he would again set foot in London.

Despite the dearth of live concerts, Dylan had been mighty busy between 1966 and 1977. He produced an astonishing run of albums: *Blonde On Blonde*, *John Wesley Harding*, *Nashville Skyline*, *Self Portrait*, *New Morning*, *Pat Garrett & Billy the Kid*, *Planet Waves*, *Blood On the Tracks*, *The Basement Tapes* and *Desire*.

Many of these albums were Gold and Platinum sellers in the UK, and it is fair to say that Dylan's popularity and respect among British fans had, unlike many other artists, not waned under the cultural onslaught of punk music that began in 1976. Steve Jones of the Sex Pistols, who might have been expected to consign Dylan to the dinosaur category, said, 'His lyrics were great. You kind of like him because he was kind of rebellious.'

Dylan's long break from touring had ended in 1974, when he went back on the road with The Band across the USA and Canada. There were no European dates, so British fans consoled themselves with playing the *Planet Waves* album, released in January. Later the same year, they could hear what they had been missing by listening to the live double album *Before the Flood*, recorded during 'Tour 74'.

In 1975, the classic album *Blood on the Tracks* was released to critical acclaim. From the summer of 1975 until 1976, Dylan trailed his next album, *Desire*, through North America and Canada, headlining the legendary Rolling Thunder Revue. London waited. He still didn't come.

Finally, in 1977, Dylan began to plan a tour that was to take in Japan, Australia and Europe. He recruited a large band, and three backing singers, but before he could start rehearsals two momentous events rocked his life. The first was his divorce from his wife Sara in February 1977, a personal and very expensive blow, and the second was the death of Elvis Presley in August of the same year, which caused him to re-evaluate his life. Adding to the pressure, Dylan was finalizing his film *Renaldo and Clara*, a four-hour-long marathon filmed during the Rolling Thunder Revue, which would eventually be released in January 1978 to a critical mauling.

The tour began in Japan, at Nippon Budokan. It was the first time Dylan had ever played in Japan, and fans treated the early gigs like a classical concert, not applauding until the very end of the set. Dylan must have been wondering what was happening and if maybe he was suffering a silent 'Judas' moment! A live album, *Bob Dylan at Budokan*, was recorded and was an extra teaser for expectant London fans.

Between finishing the Asian and Australasian leg of the world tour and coming to Europe, Dylan returned to America to record *Street-Legal*. This album spawned a rare thing in the last days of the UK's Dylan drought – a Top 20 single. The song, 'Baby, Stop Crying', was even played on BBC television's *Top Of The Pops*, set to a gyratory performance from dance troupe Legs & Co.

By the time it was announced that Dylan was to return to London in June 1978 for a series of shows at Earls Court, there was something akin to revived Dylan mania. The 16,000-seater Exhibition Centre was booked for six dates.

When he finally arrived in London in June 1978, Dylan was whisked off for a few whirlwind days with CBS press manager Elly Smith.

He went to a number of music venues. At the 100 Club he saw the reggae band Merger (and was so impressed that he would add them to the bill of his Blackbushe concert). He went to Clouds in Brixton (now closed), and to the Four Acres in Dalston. At the

Music Machine in Camden he saw Robert Gordon and Link Wray. Here, Sid Vicious of the Sex Pistols was restrained from lunging at Dylan with a knife for no apparent reason, and rock and roll tragedy was thankfully averted.

In a somewhat happier encounter, Dylan met up with Happy Traum, a folk singer friend from Dylan's home town of Woodstock who, by a beautiful symmetry, was playing at the Troubadour.

Dylan's 1978 world tour was an unknown quantity. Nobody could predict the effect his prolonged absence would have on ticket sales, despite evidence of expectation building following one successful album after another. Soon it became clear that the demand for tickets in Europe would necessitate a full tour, and not just Dylan's suggestion of a few dates in three or four large outdoor arenas.

Pretty soon it became clear that even six nights at Earls Court would be nowhere near enough. In the days before the internet, ticket buying tended to be by personal appearance and involved a lot of standing in line. Demand for the Earls Court dates had taken everybody, including promoter Harvey Goldsmith by surprise. Tickets went on sale one Monday morning at a widespread variety of locations, including Leeds, Glasgow and Liverpool.

In London there were a number of ticket outlets, including the Hammersmith Odeon, which is where the author of this chapter, then a teenage Dylan fan, found himself bedding down to sleep. Up and down the country, fans in their hundreds and thousands settled down for a night under the stars. Dylan once said: 'Some people feel the rain. Others just get wet.' That night, the heavens opened and the fans felt the rain … and got wet. In the middle of the night, the staff at Hammersmith Odeon took pity and let the drenched queuers sleep the night in the auditorium.

Fans in London waited for the gigs with a mixture of excitement and trepidation. This was a tour that had been dubbed the Alimony Tour, and which was expected by many to be just a Greatest Hits run-through, one that would struggle for critical and fan recognition. As Dylan writer Roy Kelly said, 'What would the concerts bring? After such a long absence what would he mean now?'

In reality it exceeded all expectations. A reviewer for the *Daily Mail* wrote that Dylan at Earls Court was 'the greatest concert I have ever seen'. While that might say more about the hyperbole of the reviewer than anything else, it was

> Dylan once said: 'Some people feel the rain. Others just get wet.' That night, the heavens opened and the fans felt the rain … and got wet. In the middle of the night, the staff at Hammersmith Odeon took pity and let the drenched queuers sleep the night in the auditorium.
>
> **Map ref. 12**

clear that what was happening on stage was really working.

1978 was the very eye of the bootleg storm that had begun with *Great White Wonder* in 1969, so security was tight at the Earls Court gigs. As a result, there is very little by way of audio recording and video, and indeed very few photos. What audio there is tends to be poor and hampered by the muffling of coats, but what is available reveals a vibrant Dylan with fabulous backing singers and a band as good as any that has toured with him. Billy Cross on guitar is spectacular and his combination with Steve Douglas on tenor saxophone on tracks such as 'I Don't Believe You' is sumptuous. Dylan introduces a lively 'Maggie's Farm' by saying: 'This is a song that has got me in a lot of trouble'.

Kelly wrote, 'From the back of the vastness of Earls Court we saw him slow the tempo of "I Want You" right down to conversational speed. Unexpectedly it made perfect sense. It enhanced it. It made it seem French and brought out the sadness of desire.'

Dylan paid the highest tribute to the warmth of the English audiences that year, commenting to the Earls Court audience, 'I'm glad the songs mean as much to you as they do to me … actually I'm thinking of moving to Liverpool!'

Dylan returned to Earls Court in 1981 and during the concert on the 28 June he introduced an old song, 'Mary From The Wild Moor', with a nod to his first

> Dylan paid the highest tribute to the warmth of the English audiences that year, commenting to the Earls Court audience, 'I'm glad the songs mean as much to you as they do to me ... actually I'm thinking of moving to Liverpool!'
> **Map ref. 13**

trip to London. 'We're gonna play a real old song here. A song I used to sing before I used to write any songs. I used to sing this in the Troubadour. I don't know if that club is still called the Troubadour? Well, it's the same way we used to sing it then, hasn't changed a bit.'

* * *

Tickets for Earls Court had sold out so quickly that many fans were left without. The solution to this unexpected demand came in the form of a disused air force space in Camberley, just outside London. Dylan was heading to Blackbushe.

Built in 1941, Blackbushe had three all-weather runways and was capable of taking the largest aircraft flying at that time. Proximity to the A30 apparently caused security problems, but nevertheless Blackbushe aerodrome played its part throughout the Second World War. After closure in the 1960s it enjoyed a stint as a drag racing venue during a short-lived British craze, but by 1978 it was essentially a derelict area used to hold weekend car boot sales.

Harvey Goldsmith had promoted other large outdoor events, notably the Crystal Palace garden parties. At Blackbushe, he continued the 'English Country Garden' theme – except that Blackbushe was flat and featureless and exactly what you would expect from a disused airfield. Billing the festival as The Picnic didn't fool anyone.

The stage was decorated with large silver balls on either side, and helicopters dropped *Street-Legal* badges from the sky onto the audience. Merger opened the show, and were followed by Eric Clapton, Joan Armatrading and Camberley local hero Graham Parker & the Rumour, among others.

Backstage Dylan said to Parker, 'I really love that song of yours.' After a long and anxious pause where Parker waited to hear which one, Dylan blurted out, '"Don't Ask Me Questions"!' As Parker says, 'At that moment a photo was taken and I look like I am having a great time … but I was really sweating bullets.'

The set began with an instrumental version of 'My Back Pages' and no sign of Dylan on the stage. During the last few bars, as twilight fell, he made his entrance wearing black trousers, black jacket and waistcoat and, helpfully in the days before video screens, a large top hat borrowed from a doorman at the Dorchester Hotel.

The first half of the show was largely a Greatest Hits parade but included new material from the album *Street-Legal*. Dylan's second set began with a number of solo songs from his backing singers because he said (surely in jest) that he was getting tired. Then he played an acoustic solo, 'Gates of Eden', picked out by just a spotlight, a beautiful moment in a set that was interlaced with attempted pyrotechnics. This was the 1970s, after all, and they were using Pink Floyd's rig.

The set finished with 'Señor (Tales of Yankee Power)', another song from *Street-Legal*, introduced by Dylan as being inspired by Harry Dean Stanton. 'He's in the house tonight,' said Dylan, as a spotlight picked out the actor, who took a bow. The encores finished with Eric Clapton coming on stage for 'Forever Young'. Too stoned to play lead, he just stood there grinning as Dylan told the story of the song. The final encore after five minutes of determined applause was 'The Times They Are A-Changin" – and it was all over. At three hours and five minutes, Dylan's performance at Blackbushe was his longest ever continuous appearance on stage.

Two hundred thousand fans attempted to get away. As they departed, Dylan said, 'I hope to see you real soon. I wanna come back' – and this time he meant it.

He would indeed come back real soon, a changed man.

In June 1981, when he returned to Earls Court, it was as a Christian and with a setlist that included songs from his 'Born Again' era, in particular from the album *Shot of Love*. There was no stampede for tickets and even rumours that there might be cancellations for the five shows.

Before the first gig there were a few days for the musicians and Dylan to rest in London. Writer Michael Gray relates a story told by Debbie Gold, one of the team of 'handlers' assigned to look after Dylan at all times during his time in London. On the first afternoon it became apparent that no one had seen him for a few hours. Panic that Dylan might be out in London and mobbed ensued but eventually Dylan rang in. 'Well I was feeling a little cooped up in this hotel room' he said. Dylan said that he had walked, unrecognised, around Piccadilly Circus, up and down the Kings Road and had wound up at London Zoo in Regents Park. Dylan said that he was 'just sitting quietly on a hill', enjoying the anonymity and the time away from the rock 'n' roll circus, he said that he 'didn't want the day to end'.

Eventually it was closing time and Dylan was the only visitor left in the zoo. The zookeeper walked over to the lone figure on the hill 'It's closing time. I'm afraid you're going to have to leave, Mr Dylan!'

During the 1981 Earls Court concerts, the crowd was muted and there was slow handclapping during some sets, but Dylan, the consummate performer, managed to turn things around and won some standing ovations. Throughout the gigs he was lively and animated and talked frequently to the audience. As with the Christian era albums, these Earls Court shows have been viewed kindly in retrospect, in no small part due to the release in November 2017 of the film *Trouble No More*.

Fame, fortune and even God had come to Dylan in the 19 years since he played the Troubadour, but his heart and his musical soul had not changed at all.

Chapter 8
CAMDEN TOWN AND CROUCH END

Camden Town is a vibrant north London destination and home of the world-famous Camden Market. Named after the first Earl Camden, Charles Pratt, Camden used to be the small village of 'Red Mother Cap', part of the manor of Kentish Town. For some years Mother Red Cap was the name of the area's best-known pub, one which had formerly gone by the name of Mother Damnable's, named after a woman who lived in a cottage on the site (then wasteland), ostracised and condemned as a witch after two of her associates disappeared. (The body of one was found, half-burned, in her oven.) It is now another of London's many World's Ends.

In 1791, Earl Camden began building houses on either side of the road past the pub, intending to create a place of tranquillity outside London for the educated upper and middle classes. It didn't quite work out like that. The Regents Canal opened in 1820 and so too did the warehouses and factories, especially with the arrival of the railway. Camden became an area for the working class.

The main industries that grew up were piano manufacturers, wine merchants and gin distillers. Many years later, Bob Dylan was to get the London Gin bug on his trips to the Troubadour Club.

Camden has a rich and extraordinary musical history and has both spawned and welcomed many great artists over the years. From the Rolling Stones and David Bowie, through punk to Madness and beyond, Camden has been the focal point for the London music scene. When local prodigy Amy Winehouse (who has a statue in Camden) collected her 2008 Grammy Award, she announced, 'This is for Camden! Camden Town ain't burning down!'

On 21 July 1993, without fanfare or warning, Camden found itself the location of a strange and beautiful walkabout by the greatest of them all, Bob Dylan.

The year before, Dylan had released the first of what most people believed were to be two 'contractual' albums – that is to say, albums hastily put out by an artist to fulfil a contract. The first, *Good as I Been to You*, had been a pleasant enough stroll through some traditional blues and folk numbers.

But the album released in 1993, *World Gone Wrong*, was a masterpiece (placed by no less a Dylanologist than Michael Gray in his Top 5 of Dylan albums), and Camden is forever associated with it.

Around this time, Dylan was considering a collaboration with Dave Stewart – of Eurythmics fame and also a world-renowned music producer. Ahead of his Camden walkabout, Dylan spent time with Stewart at his home and music studio, the Crypt, in Crouch End, just north of Camden Town.

Dylan even contemplated buying a house in the area. At a viewing of a semi-detached property, the owners opened the door to a tall man and a woman. Behind them was a 'little guy'. The owner later commented, 'I was a bit annoyed because they were an hour early and I told them to wait so I could get the dog out. When I realised who the little one was, I was speechless.'

During his stay in the area, he visited Banners Restaurant, still going at 21 Park Road in Crouch End. To this day music fans book and queue to have their photo taken at a small table where a brass

> During his stay in the area, he visited Banners Restaurant, still going at 21 Park Road in Crouch End. To this day music fans book and queue to have their photo taken at a small table where a brass plaque tells us: 'Bob Dylan Sat At This Table, August 1993'.
>
> **Map ref. 2**

plaque tells us: 'Bob Dylan Sat At This Table, August 1993'. Outside Banners is a huge mural of the restaurant with diners, and in one corner there is a figure who is recognisably Dylan. Beside it is a speech bubble saying: 'Don't you know who I am?' Legend has it that this is what he said when told he had to eat rather than just drink.

Banners has been run by Juliette Banner since 1992. Her then husband, the DJ Andy Kershaw, interviewed Dylan at the Crypt. Kershaw later described the interview as 'disastrous', and he joins a long list of Dylan interviewers who don't sleep well afterwards. A tip for anyone considering interviewing Dylan: don't ask him about Live Aid.[1]

Dylan's time in Crouch End also spawned one of the more bizarre of all musical urban myths.

Dave Stewart's studio was at 145 Crouch Hill. Dylan flew in from Malibu to meet up with Stewart at the address that had been written, in the era before mobile phones, on a scrap of paper. In a tragi-comic miscommunication, Dylan gave the address to the taxi driver as Crouch End Hill, a road nearby. As is the way with all good urban myths, there are a number of different versions of what happened next. We will stick with

---

1. Michael Gray called Dylan's set at Live Aid 'the most dishevelled, debilitatingly drunk performance of [Dylan's] career'. For all sorts of reasons, it is an occasion Dylan may prefer to forget.

the version we heard from the woman concerned, who phoned in her account to *The Danny Baker Show*.

Having got the address wrong, Dylan rang the doorbell of the house nearest in number to 145 in Crouch End Hill; there is no Number 145 in this road.

The woman answered the door, and came face-to-face with ... Bob Dylan. 'Is Dave here?' he asked.

Now, by chance – not, admittedly, a million-to-one chance given how many men called Dave live in North London – the woman's husband was a plumber called Dave. Bemused, but infused with English politeness, the woman explained that Dave was out but that Dylan could wait until he got back. He waited in the house with a cup of tea for some time. Eventually Dave the plumber phoned home to say he would not be long. 'Oh great,' said the woman, 'see you in a bit. Oh Dave,' she added, 'by the way ... did you invite Bob Dylan over?'

Since that time many versions of the story have made the rounds. In 2017, one version was the basis of a short film called 'Knockin' on Dave's Door' starring Eddie Marsan as a particularly enigmatic and philosophical Dylan, part of Sky Arts' *Urban Myths* series.

* * *

Once the *World Gone Wrong* album had been recorded back home in Dylan's Malibu garage studio, it just remained to find cover artwork and create a video for what was considered the standout track, 'Blood in My Eyes'.

The *World Gone Wrong* album cover is now very familiar to music fans and is arguably one of the finest of any Dylan album. It shows a sartorially elegant Dylan in a top hat, looking every inch like Earl Camden and the master of all he surveys. In the image by photographer Ana Maria Velez Wood, Dylan sits in the window seat of Flukes Cradle, a café at 275 Camden High Street. Behind him is a painting.

That painting, called *L'Etranger*, is by Irish artist Peter Gallagher. In his own words, it is a 'dour and moody portrait', showing a 'desperate and forlorn figure, on a beach having just committed a murder'. The character is in fact Meursault, from the Albert Camus novel after which Gallagher named his painting.

In 1993, in fine artistic tradition, Gallagher was unknown and impoverished. The story behind the painting is one of mystery and deceit, worthy of its own song on *World Gone Wrong*.

> Dylan sits in the window seat of Flukes Cradle, a café at 275 Camden High Street.
> **Map ref. 1**

In 1993 Peter Gallagher was exhibiting in small galleries and cafés around the country, making just enough money to starve. One of the cafés he persuaded to show his work was Flukes Cradle. *L'Etranger* hung in the café, unloved and unsold ... and then Dylan sat in front of it.

Gallagher was not a Dylan fan. Anything Dylan-related had passed him by over the decades, until one day he received a phone call from a woman wanting to buy the painting. She said that she had fallen in love with it and would pay a lot of money. Gallagher explained that because no one had been interested in it at all and he couldn't sell it, he had given the painting to a friend.

The woman was persistent, though, and they arranged to meet at Flukes Cradle on 30 October. When Gallagher arrived, he told the owner that he had a buyer for the painting. 'Oh, the one that Dylan sat under,' the owner replied. It was the first that the artist had heard of his painting's new-found fame.

The woman did then buy the painting for £500 (about £1,000 in today's values), which Gallagher split with his friend. A couple of weeks passed and Gallagher had another call, this time from his sister's boyfriend, who had seen the album *World Gone Wrong* in the window of a record shop. Over the next few days as the album was publicised, the image of his painting followed Gallagher around on huge posters plastered on walls throughout the London Underground.

Over in America it dawned on the record company executives, and their lawyers, that they had no permission from the artist to use his painting. Mild legal panic ensued. In February 1994 Gallagher was informed that Dylan, through Sony/Columbia, had bought *L'Etranger*. The enterprising woman had made a tidy profit of £2,000 (about £4,000 in today's values). Eventually the painting was returned to Gallagher with a promise that his name would be credited on future copies of the album. After time in Brazil, making award-winning short films and exhibiting in Beijing, Gallagher is now again working as an artist in North London, only a short distance away from where Dylan sat in front of his painting.

As for the photographer Ana Maria Velez Wood, she received her own life-changing phone call on the morning of 21 July 1993. Dave Stewart was a friend of hers and asked if she would like to photograph Dylan walking through Camden for a video that Stewart himself would be shooting.

Having just returned from a project in the Colombian Amazon, Ana was undaunted. Introduced to Dylan at the Crypt Studios, she remembers his handshake as 'faint'. Throughout the day, as Stewart directed the video for 'Blood in My Eyes', Ana took photos. As he walked along Camden Lock meeting fans, she took glorious pictures of Dylan resplendent in top hat and leather gloves, with a German Shepherd dog, stick in mouth, on a lead. Her photos were years later exhibited in the Testbed1 Gallery in Battersea to great acclaim.

At the end of the walkabout and back at the studio, Dave Stewart asked an engineer to fetch a guitar and

Ana sang a song in Portuguese to an attentive Dylan. Then they went for a late-night curry at a local restaurant, The Shamrat of India.

It was some time later that Ana was to find out that her photograph of Dylan in Flukes Cradle would adorn the cover of *World Gone Wrong*.

The walkabout in Camden also attracted the attention of Andrew Muir. Now a respected Dylan writer and the author of *The True Performing Of It*, comparing the careers of Dylan and Shakespeare, he was in 1993 the producer of the Dylan fanzine *Homer, the slut*, an informative and irreverent publication which ran from 1990 to 1995 but consisted of only 11 issues. On 21 July 1993 he received a telephone call from his brother-in-law. Muir was worried he might be the bearer of bad news. In fact, the call was to tell him that Dylan was at that moment strolling around Camden.

Muir did what any fan would do: he immediately left work, hailed a taxi and got on the trail. Finding that Dylan was in Flukes Cradle café, he picked up some copies of his fanzine from Compendium Bookshop (conveniently located just across the road), and then took a seat in the front of the café as Dylan ate with Dave Stewart and others, at the back. He moved from table to table, getting closer. Later he described how he felt in the moment: 'I'm still feeling pretty happy …, seeing Him so close is a big thrill. I order a drink. I sit down. I stand up. I sit down again. I move table.' Muir is every Dylan fan.

After a while the waiter, who understood what Muir was planning, said, 'Go now! Now's a good time. You'll never have a better chance in your life. Go now!'

Muir was at the point that many Dylan fans have dreamed of; the agony of the moment was intense. 'What am I going to say? I have no idea. Staying alive is barely within my grasp at this moment. Thinking stopped some time ago. I tear my tongue from the roof of my mouth. "Excuse me, Mr Dylan," I squeak.'

Muir got his autograph and talked to Dylan about his fanzine. Dylan took a copy.

Reflecting on his experience of encountering Dylan, Muir remarks, 'Even the ordinary things do not lessen the aura, the mystique. He is doing normal things, but he is set apart. I never believed such a thing possible; but he just doesn't walk and talk like anybody else. He is Bob Dylan.'

On his way back to Compendium, the euphoric Muir forgot about the traffic in Camden High Street and was lucky to escape with his life. 'Hey, watch the cars!' shouted Dylan, amid screeching tyres. Muir span round in the middle of the road and yelled back, 'What the hell does it matter now!'

The final product of the walkabout in July 1993 is the video to 'Blood in My Eyes', one of the best Dylan videos. We see him walking along Camden High Street and past Compendium Bookshop (now a shoe and souvenir shop), sitting at Flukes Cradle café and walking past the famous Camden Stores (now 'all you can eat' Chinese and Indian restaurants respectively). He crosses the bridge over the canal, followed by a travelling circus of jugglers and fans.

The video ends with Dylan walking unnoticed past a man who is oblivious to the legend brushing his shoulder on the pavement. Behind them is a poster that says 'Global Chaos' – the world gone wrong.

1993 is not generally seen as a vintage Dylan year, and maybe not even in the Top 10 years of a very long career. Nonetheless the year produced a fine Dylan album, a work of real love and soul, some great liner notes, the best video of his later career and a superb album cover. It is also a year that North London will never forget.

Afterword
DYLAN AND LONDON

In 1962 a young songwriter barely out of his teens found himself in a London music scene where the folk tradition flourished.

One wonders what would have happened if, on that first trip, Dylan had not been befriended by Martin Carthy, if he had not taken the opportunity to immerse himself in this musical tradition or if he had not met Robert Graves.

The Dylan who left London in January 1963 was permanently changed by the experience. His song writing, his singing, his confidence – all were affected by that first visit.

Martin Carthy sums it up:

> *His coming to England had an enormous impact on his music, and yet nobody's ever said it properly. He came and he learned. When he sat in all those folk clubs in 62, he was just soaking stuff up all the time. He heard Louis Killen, he heard Nigel Denver, he heard Bob Davenport, he heard me, he heard The Thameside Four, dozens of people. Anybody who came into The Troubadour, or came into the King & Queen, or the Singers' Club, and he listened and he just gobbled stuff up. The first complete album he made after he first visited England was* The Times They Are A-changin, *and England is all over that album; it's all over* Another Side of Bob Dylan *too and it's all over a large area of his work at that time.*

Dylan writer Clinton Heylin has suggested that Dylan soaked up almost as much from a single month immersed in the London folk scene as he had from the previous two years in New York.

His meeting with Robert Graves at number 9, Tregunter Road is arguably the missing part of the puzzle, an encounter which fired Dylan's literary ambitions and propelled him into a whole new level of song writing to sit alongside the increased depth of confidence he acquired as a musician. Without that meeting, would the Nobel Prize for literature, finally presented in 2017 (there was an earlier attempt twenty years previously led by Allen Ginsburg), have ever become a reality?

Throughout his career London has acted as both a spark and a support for Dylan. Dylan has written classic songs in London from *Girl from the North Country* in 1962 through to the 'long piece of vomit' begun at the Savoy and Queen Mary's Hospital which became *Like A Rolling Stone*, and beyond. In London Dylan made the first commercially successful music video, set the benchmark for the music film, and even in 1978 with the Picnic in the Park at Blackbushe, kickstarted the modern music festival.

London was the first tentative step out in to the world for a young Bob Dylan. And it was the perfect melting pot out of which he would emerge as an artist who would go on to conquer the world. London will always have the honour of being the city which forged the greatest of modern songwriters.

LIST OF ILLUSTRATIONS

1. Royal Albert Hall
2. 9 Tregunter Road
3. Savoy Steps
4. Camden
5. Dylan Map of London
6. Blackbushe
7. Folk Clubs
8. Savoy Hotel
9. May Fair Hotel

All illustrations © Julia Wytrazek.

LOCATIONS LIST

Performed

Troubadour, Earls Court
Dylan performed here twice, 29 December 1962 and 12 January 1963

King & Queen, Foley Street, Fitzrovia
Performs here 21 December 1962, first ever performance outside USA

Pindar of Wakefield (now the Water Rats), Kings Cross (Singers' club)
Performs here 22 December 1962

BBC Studios (Aldwych)
Recording in December 1962 of play *Madhouse on Castle Street*

Dobells Jazz and Folk Record Shop, Charing Cross Road
Dylan records as Blind Boy Grunt on Eric Von Schmidt album, 14 January 1963

Embassy Club, Soho
Club where a 1963 review mentions that Dylan played a short set

Royal Festival Hall, South Bank
Plays one night here 17 May 1964, concert is sold out

Royal Albert Hall, Kensington Gore
Plays here first in May 1965, returning in 1966, 2013 and 2015

Savoy Steps, Embankment Gardens and Savoy hotel
Three locations where DA Pennebaker shot film for 'Subterranean Homesick Blues' on 8 May 1965; Savoy Steps was chosen as the introduction to the final cut of *Dont Look Back*

BBC Studios (Shepherds Bush)
On 1 June 1965 Dylan performed at the BBC studios in Shepherds Bush. He performed a full setlist which included 'Ballad of Hollis Brown', 'Mr Tambourine Man', 'It Ain't Me Babe' and 'It's All Over Now, Baby Blue'. The performance was broadcast over two nights, 19 and 26 June

Queen's Gate Mews, Kensington SW7
Dylan stands in front of a sign that says 'We will collect, clip, bath and return your dog' and skits a surreal verse based on the words. The clip, filmed in 1966 for *Eat the Document*, appears in Martin Scorcese's documentary film about Dylan, *No Direction Home*, released in 2012

Earls Court Arena
In 1978 plays his first London dates for 12 years. Plays six nights. Returns to Earls Court in 1981 for a further six nights

Blackbushe
In 1978, Dylan plays for 200,000 people at the Picnic in the Park outdoor music festival just a short distance from London

Wembley Arena
The *Temples in Flame* tour with Tom Petty and the Heartbreakers finished with four nights here in October 1987. Plays here in October 1987 for four nights and returns again in 1989, 1997, 1998, 2000, 2003 and 2017

Wembley Stadium
In 1984 in his largest gig since the Isle of Wight in 1969, Dylan played on a bill with, amongst many others, Van Morrison, Eric Clapton and Mick Jagger

Shepherds Bush Empire
Plays here in 2003

Finsbury Park
Location of the only UK Dylan show of the summer of 2011

Levy's Recording Studio, Regent Street
Attempts to record with John Mayall's Bluesbreakers, including Eric Clapton, on 12 May 1965. Session collapses

Church Studio, Crouch End
Records parts of 20 songs at Dave Stewart's studio. Session is a shambles

London Townhouse Studios, Shepherds Bush
A ramshackle session for the film *Hearts of Fire*, directed by Richard Marquand, took place 27 and 28 August 1986

Heaven Nightclub, Charing Cross
One scene for the film *Hearts of Fire* shot in 1986

Shepperton Studios
Main venue for the film *Hearts of Fire* during 1986

Electric Ballroom, Camden
In 1986 Dylan plays concert scene for *Hearts of Fire* in front of 300 punks

Hammersmith Odeon
Dylan plays six nights here in 1990, returning for a further eight nights in 1991

Hyde Park
Played in 1996 for the Prince's Trust Charity and in 2019 where he was joined on the bill by Neil Young

London Palladium
Dylan finally played this famous venue in 2017

Stayed

May Fair Hotel
Stays here briefly in 1962 and returns in 1966 where a very fed-up Dylan is filmed by Fiona Adams and

interviewed by Max Jones of the *Melody Maker*. The article that is published is entitled *Will the Real Bob Dylan Please Stand Up*

Philip Saville's house, Hampstead
Stays here in 1962, performs 'Blowin' in the Wind' for Saville's au pairs

Martin Carthy's house, 184 Haverstock Hill. Beside Belsize Park
Stays here in 1962, helps chop up piano for firewood

Savoy Hotel, Embankment
Base for Dylan during 1965 UK tour. Backdrop to *Dont Look Back* filmed by DA Pennebaker

Royal Gardens Hotel, Kensington
Stays here during 1978 UK tour

Clubs

Bunjies Coffee House, Litchfield Street, Soho
Visited several times in 1962

Les Cousins, Greek Street, Soho
Visited during first trip in 1962 and then again with Alan Price in 1965

The Establishment Club, Greek Street, Soho
Visited in late 1962

Roundhouse Pub, Wardour Street, Soho
Dylan visits in December 1962 with Martin Carthy

Surbiton and Kingston Folk Club
Visits in January 1963

Cromwellian Club, Mayfair
Dylan visits with the Rolling Stones and Beatles, 1966

Marquee Club, Wardour Street
Reportedly plays with Lee Hazelwood on 11 May 1965

Music Machine, Camden
Watches Robert Gordon Band including Link Wray in June 1978

100 Club, Oxford Street
Sees reggae band Merger in June 1978 and adds them to the bill at Blackbushe

Dingwalls, Camden
Watches George Thoroughgood and the Destroyers in June 1978. Returns in 1985 to see Hugh Masekela

Place Next Door, Covent Garden
Attends CBS party in June 1978

Four Aces Club, Dalston
Visits in June 1978

Empress of Russia Folk Club, Islington
In 1987, Dylan turns up in disguise to watch the Campbell family play

Cafes and restaurants

Star Cafe, Soho
Coffee shop where Dylan discussed *The White Goddess* with Hans Fried

Flukes Cradle cafe, Camden High Street
Location of photo shoot for *World Gone Wrong* took place on 21 July 1993

Banners, Crouch End
Cafe which Dylan visited in August 1993, marked with a bronze plaque at 'his' table. See also the mural on the outside wall.

The Shamrat of India, Crouch End
Indian restaurant in Crouch End that Dylan allegedly frequented with Dave Stewart during the summer of 1993

Other

Office of *Melody Maker*, Fleet Street
December 1962, Dylan tries and fails to meet journalist Max Jones

9 Tregunter Road
Meets Robert Graves at party here in January 1963

Heathrow Airport
Arrival in 1965 recorded in *Dont Look Back* and the 'lightbulb' interview is recorded in the VIP Lounge

Kenwood, Hampstead
Dylan visits John Lennon in May 1965

St Mary' Hospital, Paddington
Falling ill at the Savoy Hotel Dylan briefly checks in during May 1965

Friar Park, Henley on Thames
October 1987 Dylan spends time with George Harrison at Harrison's home just outside London. In the grounds of the house are caves, grottoes, underground passages, a multitude of garden gnomes, and an Alpine rock garden with a scale model of the Matterhorn

Camden Town
In July 1993 Dylan went walkabout through Camden Town for the video *Blood In My Eyes*. The cover picture for *World Gone Wrong* was taken in Flukes Cradle Café on Camden High Street

Old Vic
Dylan offers access to any of his songs for the playwright Conor McPherson to put together a stage play, which he did with the composer and arranger Simon Hale. *Girl from the North Country* opened at the Old Vic on 8 July 2017. It returned twice to the West End and won two Olivier awards. In 2020 the play moved to Broadway.

BIBLIOGRAPHY

White Goddess: A Historical Grammar of Poetic Myth, Robert Graves (Faber & Faber, 1948)

Kral Majales, Allen Ginsberg (City Lights, 1968)

Bob Dylan, Anthony Scaduto (Grossat & Dunlap, 1971)

Bob Dylan in his own words, compiled by Miles (Omnibus, 1978)

No Direction Home: The Life and Music of Bob Dylan, Robert Shelton (New English Library, 1986)

'A conversation with… Martin Carthy', Dave Brazier (*The Telegraph Magazine*, No. 42, Summer 1992)

Faithfull: An Autobiography, Marianne Faithfull (Little Brown, 1994)

Touched by the Hand of Bob, Dave Henderson (Black Book Company, 1995)

Like the Night, CP Lee (Helter Skelter Publishing, 1998)

Positively 4th Street: The Lives and Times of Joan Baez, Bob Dylan, Mimi Baez Farina and Richard Farina, David Hajdu (Farrer Strauss and Giraiux, 2001)

The Razors Edge: Bob Dylan & the Neverending Tour, Andrew Muir (Helter Skelter Publishing, 2001)

Chronicles: Volume 1, Bob Dylan (Simon & Schuster, 2004)

And a Voice to Sing With: A Memoir, Joan Baez (Simon & Schuster, 2009)

D.A. Pennebaker, Keith Beattie (University of Illinois Press, 2011)

Once Upon a Time: The Lives of Bob Dylan, Ian Bell (Mainstream Publishing, 2013)

Singing from The Floor: A History of British Folk Clubs, JP Bean (Faber & Faber, 2014)

The Story of Mayfair: From 1664 onwards, Peter Wetherell, Erik Brown and Oliver Bradbury (Wetherell, 2014)

Bob Dylan Dream: My Life with Bob, Roy Kelly (Pembury House Publishing, 2015)

The Hurdy Gurdy Man, Donovan Leitch (Donovan Prints, 2016)

Humdinger Folk Singer: The Story of Judas and the Communists, Derek Barker (ISIS, 2016)

'Bob Dylan – The real Royal Albert Hall 1966 Concert, Steve Ricciutti (*SoundBlab*, https://soundblab.com/reviews/albums/16759-bob-dylan-the-real-royal-albert-hall-1966-concert, 2016)

Why Dylan Matters, Richard F. Thomas (William Collins, 2017)

Testimony, Robbie Robertson (Windmill Books, 2017)

Friends and Other Strangers: Bob Dylan Examined, Harold Lepidus (Oakmoor Publishing, 2017)

Time Out of Mind: The Lives of Bob Dylan, Ian Bell (Pegasus, 2017)

Bob Dylan and the British Sixties: A Cultural History, Tudor Jones (Routledge, 2018)

Bob Dylan & Shakespeare: The True Performing of It, Andrew Muir (Red Planet, 2019)

Bob Dylan: Outlaw Blues, Spencer Leigh (McNidder & Grace, 2020)

Additional Resources

www.thesavoylondon.com/

www.camden.gov.uk/

City A.M., https://www.cityam.com/ (22 December 2014)

ACKNOWLEDGEMENTS

We wish to acknowledge the following, without whose help, support and contributions *Bob Dylan in London* would be little more than the ramblings of two Dylan fans.

Julia Wytrazek for her beautiful illustrations. From the first sketch we knew she had the vision to bring *Bob Dylan in London* to life.

Tony Benjamin for his dedication and patience in editing *Bob Dylan in London*. His determination to root out hyperbole, repetition and verbiage was never overbearing, but always spot on.

Robert Penney for his important contribution to the cover design, and his enthusiastic support for both the Dylan Room at the Troubadour and *Bob Dylan in London*.

Caroline Curtis, for pushing the book to the next level, through ruthless but completely fair comments and suggestions. But above all for recognising the fun we'd had writing it.

Chris Symes, for sharing her memories of seeing Bob Dylan playing at the Royal Albert Hall in both 1965 and 1966. What we wouldn't give to have been there too.

Susan Scott from the Savoy Hotel for clarifying the remodelling of the hotel in 1910. So sad that the pandemic prevented a face-to-face meeting and tour but we'll be there when they restart.

Ian Williamson and all the staff at the Troubadour for supporting the launch of the Dylan Room at the Troubadour, a space which numerous Dylan fans in London have now visited and been inspired, and where we spent many happy hours planning and talking about Dylan in London.

The Dylan Band: Fred Ward, Steve Heath, Steve Greenwood, Matt Withey and Ronnie Paris, for keeping the spirit of Bob Dylan alive in London.

Andrew Muir for his contributions and for writing such a brilliant foreword to *Bob Dylan in London*.

Stephanie Audhali, **Sotiris Kyriacou** and **Atalanta Kernick**, for their encouragement and for making Cubitt Town library such a welcoming space to write in.

For wise Dylan counsel and inspiration, Michael Gray, Malcolm Barr Hamilton, Ken Hunt, Harold Lepidus, Anne Margaret Daniel, Laura Tenschert, Gareth Davies, Adam Scott-Goulding, Hans Buskes, Richard Thomas, Richard Foster, and Eclectica Podcast.

And finally, Andy and Caroline Peden Smith at McNidder & Grace for their faith in the stories and their tireless help in bringing it all together.

FORTHCOMING

Bob Dylan in the Big Apple: Troubadour Tales of New York
by K G Miles
ISBN 9780857162205
Publication date November 2021

AUTHOR BIOGRAPHIES

Jackie Lees first heard Bob Dylan sing 'Lay Lady Lay' on the radio when she was 13, and went out the next day to track down more from the owner of *that* voice. Around 40 years later she went on a Dylan pilgrimage through London with co-author K G Miles, and realised that a guidebook would mean other fans could do the same. A career of writing and editing for a homelessness charity was interrupted to co-curate the Dylan Room at the Troubadour, to provide amateur management for the Dylan Band and to write *Bob Dylan in London: Troubadour Tales*.

K G Miles. From an awestruck child at the Isle of Wight Festival in 1969 to the honour of addressing the inaugural conference at the Tulsa Archive in 2019, Bob Dylan has taken Londoner K G Miles on an emotional musical journey lasting over 50 years. Now, as co-curator of the Dylan Room at London's Troubadour Club, through writing, podcasts and Dylan tours, K G Miles is able to share his knowledge and experience with music lovers throughout the world.